"IT'S NOT ENOUGH FOR YOUR DOCTOR TO STOP PLAYING GOD. YOU'VE GOT TO GET OFF YOUR KNEES."

We hesitate to question the doctor. We're afraid to intervene. And this, ironically, endangers our lives. Medical work requires constant input. But the combination of awe and fright so overwhelms our ability to communicate events, emotions, and the sheer facts of illness that patients unconsciously hold back vital information that's critical to their medical care. The doctor, in turn, may not be aware of the information he isn't getting. Such ignorance produces medical tragedies.

THIS BOOK UNVEILS THE MEDICAL MYSTIQUE AND PUTS YOU IN CHARGE OF MAKING THE DECISIONS THAT ARE SO IMPORTANT TO YOUR LIFE.

"IT IS ESSENTIAL READING FOR ALL PEOPLE WHO VALUE THEIR OWN GOOD HEALTH."

—Barbara Seaman,
author of *FREE AND FEMALE*

Beyond the Medical Mystique

How to Choose
and Use
Your Doctor

*The Smart Patient's Way
to a Longer, Healthier Life*

by Marvin S. Belsky, M.D.,

and Leonard Gross

A FAWCETT CREST BOOK

Fawcett Publications, Inc., Greenwich, Connecticut

HOW TO CHOOSE & USE YOUR DOCTOR

THIS BOOK CONTAINS THE COMPLETE TEXT OF THE ORIGINAL HARDCOVER EDITION.

A Fawcett Crest Book reprinted by arrangement with Arbor House

Copyright © 1975 by Marvin S. Belsky, M.D., and Leonard Gross

Main Selection of the Prevention Book Club
Alternate Selection of the Book-of-the-Month-Club
Selection of the Macmillan Book Clubs

ISBN 0–449–22966–1

Printed in the United States of America

1 2 3 4 5 6 7 8 9 10

For Miriam, Ann and Paul

and for Ralph Gold

THIS BOOK could literally not have been written without the patients from whom I've learned so much. To them, my heartfelt gratitude.

I owe a debt, as well, to those physicians I have known who practice medicine as teachers as well as healers by encouraging their patients to participate actively in a truly humanistic relationship. They inspired me to try to do the same.

I am indebted also to the New York University Medical Center Library whose resources provided a continuing source of knowledge in a stimulating milieu; and to the Scientists' Institute for Public Information whose philosophy and work have been an inspiration.

Finally, I am deeply grateful to Raymond Belsky, Dr. Harry Sands, Judith and Philip Parkas and Gerald Browne for their continuing encouragement and support.

Contents

----

5 Patient Talk

A Note from Leonard Gross

WHEN a writer helps another person write a book, his work is made much easier if he believes not only that this person's argument makes sense but also that what he is saying needs to be said. My belief in this instance could hardly be more unequivocal: although I am the book's co-author, I am one of those for whom it was written. I haven't been a sufficiently critical patient. I have held doctors in awe, treated them as gods, accepted their judgments without question. Such questions as I did ask were not ample or searching or tough enough. I have chosen doctors without method and taken medicine without inquiry into its possible side effects. In sum, I have abdicated to the experts and forfeited my rights as a patient. I know now that most Americans are like me in this regard. If they're lucky, they get away with it. I wasn't lucky. Some years ago I underwent exploratory surgery that made sense at the time but wound up doing great harm and no good. Now that I have written this book with Dr. Marvin Belsky, I could not make such a mistake again. What he says has needed saying for a long time. For my sake, I wish it had been said years ago. For your sake, I'm glad it's being said at last.

Introduction

THIS BOOK takes aim at a belief that can endanger your health: an almost universally held faith and unquestioning trust in the wisdom of the doctor. We call it the "medical mystique."

The relationship between doctor and patient is as serious a problem in medicine today as are disease and ignorance.

Many patients either fear their doctors or hold them in such unrealistic high esteem that they can't communicate freely. They worry that they're wasting the doctor's time. Or, God forbid, they're boring him. For whatever reason, they don't do an adequate job of telling the doctor what's wrong with them. This failure by patients to articulate their feelings prevents the doctor from prescribing adequate care and achieving therapeutic success.

The responsibility for this failure is both the patient's and the doctor's. If patients deify their doctors, it is because we are all—doctors and patients alike—conditioned to accept an outmoded belief in the sacrosanct expert in all fields.

When the patient abdicates responsibility to the mysterious, powerful, all-knowing doctor, his survival is threatened. His well-meant faith distorts and frustrates the very function of the patient-physician relationship, drains it of humanity.

If a person is to live as long and as well as he should, he must know everything he can possibly know about his medical condition. It is neither right nor helpful for the doctor *and* the patient to suppose that only the doctor can understand matters vital to health and long life. The patient has an enormous capacity to judge his own condition and participate in his care.

This book is a prescription for a new kind of patient: assertive, questioning, capable of making the decisions that are vital to his survival. The physician informs, the patient decides.

For such a patient to materialize, mystery and power must be removed from the medical sanctuary. In their place needs to be the kind of warmth and communication that protects and extends life.

The demystification of the medical mystique is a job for both doctor and patient. The assertive, informed patient must identify and join with those doctors who want to do away with the priestly, authoritarian aspects of the mystique. The competent, caring patient is as essential to this enterprise as is the competent, caring physician.

New technology has given powers to medicine that were scarcely imaginable twenty years ago. We can transplant organs, invade the brain, even postpone death. Doctors alone cannot and should not determine when to summon this technology. Patients can be partners in the process of determination—competent, informed exponents of their fate.

The delivery of medical care in the United States today is undergoing a process of fundamental reappraisal. New laws and new forms will undoubtedly come into being. All of us may soon be covered by National Health Insurance. Health-maintenance organizations—known as HMOs—are gaining popularity. Doctors are increasingly undergoing periodic competency reviews by their peers. But all such new forms and procedures deal primarily with the economics and technology of medical care, not its humanity or capacity for partnership between doctor and patient.

Quality care requires a secure economic basis and the very best technology. But quality care depends on concerned, humanistic communication. Without it, the doctor is handicapped and the patient endangered.

The combination of exotic new technology and bureaucratic forms of medical delivery make an effective doctor-patient partnership more urgent than ever. Unless the patient learns to participate in his own health enterprise, his care will become more and more depersonalized and remote.

How doctors and patients together can achieve this working partnership has been my preoccupying concern for the last twelve years.

I'm a physician to my marrow. I live, breathe, eat, and love medicine. I become so immersed in what I do that it permeates my being. Given the totality of the medical existence—commitment, responsibility and effort to replenish knowledge—it's little wonder that the physician believes he is more capable than anyone of understanding the problems brought to him. This is precisely the danger point. He is not wrong, but he is not complete. He will understand only what he knows. If he doesn't know all he should, his treatment will be inadequate. Not only will he not fully recognize the physical and emotional state of his patients, he will not comprehend how they feel about him—which affects how well they take his advice and treatment.

I found that out a dozen years ago when I discovered that some of my patients had failed to follow my recommendations. We simply hadn't reached one another. I determined to correct that.

I had always been interested in psychology and at one point had considered becoming a psychiatrist. Then, after more than fifteen years as an internist, I went back to school. I took courses in psychology, medical sociology, behavioral science, education, communications, and group dynamics. I made up my mind to learn from my patients by presenting myself to them under circumstances entirely different from the usual ones for doctors and patients. My thought was to create a climate in which they could tell me what they really thought about doctors, medical care, hospitals, costs, and the behavior of "gatekeepers"—the doctor's support personnel. I wanted to know what frightened them and what reassured them, what motivated them to care for themselves and what discouraged them from doing so, and above all, what they liked and didn't like about our relationship. Thus began the "feedback" sessions that have so totally changed my understanding of the doctor-patient relationship—sessions that are the foundation of this book.

The meetings have been under way for several years. They are held two times a month in the waiting room of my office in New York City. They involve five to eight patients, and myself. We meet at 7:00 P.M., after dinner, and talk for three hours. The patients discuss what most of them have never dared verbalize before: their fears, uncertainties, grievances, needs.

They are all, of course, my patients. But all of them were patients of other doctors before coming to me. Some began with pediatricians, of whom their memories are quite vivid. All were once cared for by their family doctors. At some point they moved away to set up families of their own; each move meant a new doctor, or several doctors: family physicians, internists, obstetricians, pediatricians, other specialists. Their experience has not been just with me but with hundreds of doctors from all parts of the United States.

By the standards of social science, the sample I've worked with is a fairly large one. I have more than a thousand patients; nearly half of them have now attended one or more of my so-called feedback sessions; their economic, social, and cultural backgrounds make up a most interesting cross section of American life. The attitudes they have revealed offer information not only about my own practice, but about the practices of many doctors over many years. To my knowledge, no other physician has had continuing feedback encounters with patients. What I have learned has profoundly touched me, and had a great impact on my work. I hope it has made me a better doctor—but I know for certain that it has immeasurably improved the ability and willingness of my patients to articulate their problems and be true working partners in their care.

One of the suspicions these experiences have confirmed for me is how inexpertly many people select their doctors. Next to choosing a mate, choosing a doctor is the most fateful decision we make. Yet we make it without preparation or knowledge. We go to a doctor because he has been recommended by someone no more capable than we are of making an informed judgment. Once we are with the doctor we don't determine, except in the most rudimentary way, whether we're receiving good treatment. Our inability to judge can lead to needless expense of both time and money and, in some cases, to needless suffering. The choice of doctor can be a question of life and death.

No professional in our society remains so unassailable as the doctor. "For at least 20,000 years, man has placed the healer in a special role," the report of the 1973 Pacific Medical Center Symposium on the Medical Mystique noted, "both honored and feared and almost always cloaked in mystery. The same mystique prevails today. The social status, special privilege, money and freedom from controls granted by the society tells the modern healer that he is behaving in an appropriate manner. Is he? The mystique which has grown up around the medical profession in the United States, and an analysis of its nature and implications for both professionals and laymen, are increasingly high in the national consciousness."

Articles in newspapers, testimony before Congress and the responses of the various medical societies indicate the presence of an unorganized but formidable movement for patients' rights in the United States. Underlying that movement are feelings that have been sensed but unarticulated by most Americans—that something is wrong with the delivery of health care in this country. It is too remote, too impersonal, too untouchable.

If you share any or all of these feelings, this book aspires to help you. It will familiarize you with your rights as a patient, and show you how to assert them. It will orient and guide you to better treatment. It will seek to demystify and decantify the medical mystique.

One of my first procedures with new patients is to submit myself to an examination. "Why did you choose me as your doctor?" I begin. Most of them say they were referred by a friend. "How do you know I'm a good doctor?" I ask them. The question almost always perplexes them, and invariably surprises them. It shouldn't. Finding out whether your doctor is a good one really *is* a question of life or death. You have the right to know about his qualifications, training, continuing competence, availability, the hospital he's affiliated with, his practice regarding house calls, and any and all other pertinent matters.

At the same time, you have obligations as a patient. You must know how to be a good one (which is to say a smart one). It is not just a matter of presenting yourself to your doctor when you're ill. It's knowing how and what to tell him, and being able to do so.

Faulty communication between physician and patient wastes the time and effort of both, leads to treatment on the basis of inadequate information, causes needless patient dissatisfaction. The communication gap and educational vacuum between physician and patient is the most serious and significant impediment to their therapeutic relationship. What does the patient expect of his doctor? What does the doctor expect of his patient? Until they understand one another, their relationship will be unsuccessful.

This book tries to offer a blueprint for that understanding. It identifies the deficiencies both doctors and patients bring to their relationship. It proposes remedies for those deficiencies.

If you want more from your relationship with your doctor, you don't have to wait for the millenium to get it. Even if you have no scientific or medical background whatever, you can learn how to choose a doctor, how to get more out of your relationship with your present doctor, how to ask him questions, how to identify your problems, how to handle your doctor's gatekeepers, and how to humanize your relationship.

All physicians support the objective of a better doctor-patient relationship. I am sure they will appreciate and understand the candor with which I address myself to that objective.

1

The Medical Mystique

A MYSTIQUE is an aura of mystery or mystical power surrounding a particular occupation or pursuit. It implies the existence of special, mysterious knowledge that only chosen people can possess. Only those who possess such knowledge, it follows, have the right to act in special ways.

Expertise endows the experts with qualities beyond reach of nonexperts. The experts become convinced that their special knowledge permits them to make unilateral decisions. Those whom the decisions affect are expected to accede without question. Informed self-reliance is not even considered.

A mystique can have positive helpful aspects. A loving father and mother invoke the parental mystique to make their child mindful of dangers. A man of God invokes the religious mystique to comfort the bewildered and bereaved. A concerned physician invokes the medical mystique to persuade a patient to care for himself and enhance and prolong his life.

But a mystique of any kind suffers from misuse. Parents can overprotect a child, permit him no independent decision, and deprive him of the emotional growth that enables him to develop into a self-reliant adult. Men of God can ascribe such powers to the Almighty that mortals await the will of divine intervention and do nothing to order their own lives. And doctors can so overwhelm patients that they are incapable of acting in their own interests to safeguard their health and treat their illnesses.

If you abdicate to the experts, then the medical profession is accountable to no one. Patients often feel that they are not able to judge or evaluate. That's not so. Granted, there's an unequal relationship between doctor and patient. Your doctor has specific knowledge you don't have. But you have critical faculties. You have feelings that are constantly confirmed by experience. You can judge the difference between a good meal and a bad meal, a good car ride and a bad one. You don't have to be a mechanic to appreciate the difference between a Model-T and a Cadillac.

You have to trust yourself, and have confidence in your own experiences. When you go on an airplane, you can make certain judgments, even though you're not a pilot. You know whether the airplane takes off smoothly and lands smoothly. You can judge the efficiency of the crew. You witness the dispatch with which you're discharged on landing. You can get the same feel of excellence— or nonexcellence—in a doctor's office or the hospital in which he practices.

When you go to any doctor for the first time, you see a process unfolding different from any other you've experienced. This doctor's thoroughness, the intensiveness of his involvement with your history, the logic of his approach can all be compared to such qualities in other doctors. You can begin to judge the technical element of the experience, and you can always judge the humanistic element. *You know when you're treated badly.*

The greatest problem for the patient who wants to judge his doctor is not the acquisition of experience, education, and information. It is the acquisition of a willingness to judge. Patients in the thrall of the medical mystique are unwilling to examine their doctors.

The first objective, then, is to puncture the myths of the medical mystique. Dr. Eliot Freidson, professor of sociology at New York University, lists six. The first is that the doctor is always saving the life of every patient he sees. That is simply not so. Most illness does not involve life and death, which means that many elements of judgment and training are not all that arcane.

A second element of the modern medical mystique is that medicine is a precise, effective science. The truth is that it's neither precise nor effective on many occasions; to the contrary, it may be imprecise and ineffective.

A third rationalization of the mystique is that judgment is so complex in medicine that the physician exercising it can't, himself, be judged. Not so—the diagnosing physician is often comparing symptoms to criteria that may be as basic and fixed as multiplication tables. To be a good diagnostician, he has to know his fundamentals.

The fourth is that doctors are perpetually rational. This assumes that doctors are immune to human frailties, that they don't get tired or lose their edge. Doctors *are* human. They *do* get tired. Their interest *does* flag.

A fifth aspect of the mystique is that the quality of medical work is "assured by a long, arduous course of professional training." Actually, much of what was learned may be forgotten. Doctors' knowledge becomes stale. It requires constant replenishment through continuing education.

Finally the medical mystique assumes that doctors comprise a responsible, organized profession dedicated to the public good. The truth is that dedication is variable, and doctors are no more or less dedicated than members of other professions.

I don't mean to suggest that all doctors behave as authoritarians. Only some do. But all doctors function within a tradition that may set them apart from the rest of society. They are fathers and their patients are children, and the dependency relationship hurts doctors and patients alike.

The dyadic relationship between a doctor and patient *should*—and can—involve affection, respect, admiration, and even love. The patient should have the confidence that with his doctor's help he can know more and more about his body, and the way modern medicine functions.

Most doctors are unaware of their inability to communicate or educate. They don't know what healers they could be if they could relate to their patients more profoundly, encouraging them to talk, learning about their fears and troubles as a prerequisite for quality care. If they are unwilling to take the time to hear about fears and troubles, they have failed as doctors. Fears and troubles are often the causes of psychosomatic illnesses. They are cries for help.

The charismatic mission history has given doctors to be teachers, leaders, and guardians of public concerns has not been fulfilled by doctors. It's time that it was. Medical knowledge, until now, has been disease-oriented. It's time that it was health-oriented.

Doctors today have become instruments of social control. They have been delegated ethical decision-making in matters of organ transplants, death, and psychosurgery. Their influence permeates the food and drug industries. They command life-giving arsenals. And yet, with all this power, they are accountable only to one another, because the mystique contains their knowledge within the medical sanctuary.

This is a time for accounting in America. All of our professions and institutions have come under an iconoclastic public scrutiny without parallel in our history. Within this movement there is an amorphous but impressive clamor for patients' rights: to be informed, to be seen, to be treated with consideration, to be a partner in one's own health enterprise.

It's not enough for the doctor to stop playing God. *You've* got to get off your knees. The best advocate of patients' rights is you yourself, not committees or laws or health and welfare programs. The best relationship is the simplest relationship, between doctor and patient, a questioning, assertive, well-informed patient.

ORIGINS OF THE MYSTIQUE

The medical mystique is as old as humanity. It began at some undated moment when one primitive man found a bark that helped ease the pain of another. The bark contained quinine, but he didn't know that. All he knew was that it helped. He hid his ignorance, as well as the location of the bark.

But his power to ease pain became legend and elevated him to a position of eminence in his community. To consolidate his position, he invested his cure with ceremony.

There was one additional element to the mystique of the earliest medicine man that served to compound the mystery and enhance his power. If one person's physical condition or actions became abnormal, there had to be an explanation for it as well as a way to make him normal again. Since religion, in a sense, is an attempt by man to explain a phenomenon for which he is not otherwise able to account, such restoration took on religious aspects. The power to heal centered on the *shaman,* or medicine man. To him was attached an importance over and above his human abilities. From him his patients expected miracles.

The evolution of the medical mystique reveals much of the story of civilization in the manner of excavations from an archaeological dig. The magical artifacts of the medicine man—fetishes, totems, taboos—gradually gave way to the rational approach of the Greek physicians. Hippocrates enunciated an oath that categorized the physician's responsibilities to his profession and patients. The Bible sanctified the doctor's function. The Dark Ages shrouded medicine in mysticism. With the Renaissance and the Age of Enlightenment came the evolution of the scientific method, further deepening the feelings of specialness and separateness.

The connection through all of these stages was the inherent qualities originally invested in medicine by society: the qualities of the priest, the father and the all-knowing, authoritarian deity. These characteristics persist today.

From the outset the medical mystique developed two separate elements—one constructive, the other destructive. The positive embodied the love, help, compassion, and concern that the shaman and his successors gave to the people in their care. The harmful were the fear and barriers erected and the worship, deference, obedience, and awe doctor-priests came to expect as a function of their office. The doctor-patient relationship became one that was based, at least in part, on elitism, to which the patient submitted.

The problem today is to retain the healing aspects of the mystique while at the same time reducing the doctor's domination over the patient. It is a problem for both you and the doctor. You both share responsibility for perpetuation of the mystique. If you accept your doctor's judgment without question, you are not a self-serving patient any more than an authoritarian doctor is a helping doctor. You must both work together.

Let's begin with the doctor.

The doctor today is the shaman of yesterday. He has inherited all of the medicine man's mystique, magic, and power. As the medicine man was set apart in a position of honor in society; as he gained certain cultural sanctions unique to his office; as his word had weight that would not accrue even to a tribal chief; so today the doctor is a man set apart in society. As Dr. Thomas S. Szasz, professor of psychiatry at the State University of New York, Upstate Medical Center, has said, "Formerly when religion was strong and science weak, men mistook magic for medicine. Now when science is strong and religion is weak, men mistake medicine for magic."

Obviously the power of the contemporary doctor greatly exceeds that of the medicine man. It is the power not only of reprieving life, but of enhancing it.

Most medicine men inherited their positions; power passed from father to son. The sons had the right to the position, but also the obligation of learning the ritual that went with it. Much of that ritual concerned itself with the mystique that was a significant element of the "healing" process. The medicine man's effectiveness was largely a consequence of the belief he engendered in his patients that they *would* be cured.

Young people in medical schools today—many of them the sons and daughters of physicians—are the bearers of a tradition embodying both the healing aspect and priestly aspect of the medical mystique.

There is much to be said for a healing relationship that is as old as humanity. There is much about the healing process that functions apart from medical technology. To this extent the medical mystique, as a vehicle of the physician's concern and even love for his patient, is an invaluable component of care. There are, of course, many dedicated physicians today who utilize their patient's reverence with sensitivity and skill, and, in so doing, assist the healing process. And there are too many who don't.

FEAR OF TALKING

There's a critical psychological problem for the doctor-patient relationship, however: one of its partners is frightened. It's one thing to talk about your occupation; it's another to talk about your life. We hesitate to question the doctor. We're afraid to intervene. And this, ironically, endangers life. Medical work requires constant input. But the combination of awe and fright so overwhelms the ability to communicate events, emotions, and the sheer facts of illness that patients unconsciously hold back vital information that's critical to their medical care. The doctor, in turn, may not be aware of the information he isn't getting. Such ignorance produces medical tragedies. One was recounted in a feedback session at my office.

A man in his middle fifties had suffered from a

hiatus hernia. Such a hernia occurs when gas pockets up in the chest, above the diaphragm.

Pain and discomfort in the chest may reflect gastric disturbance in the abdomen. The patient had noted all of his symptoms to his doctor. The doctor had done all the proper things: taken a history, made a physical examination, performed the appropriate laboratory tests, identified the symptoms, and made a correct diagnosis. When the patient returned for another examination, his condition was unchanged. He went home, reassured. Over the next few days, his condition began to deteriorate. He suspected that something was awry. But because his doctor had assured him that there had been no change, he decided that "doctor knows best." Who was he to question the doctor? Five days later, he suffered a collapse of his blood pressure and was rushed to the hospital. A week later he died of a massive heart attack. There was an additional cause of death: the awe that prevented him from supplying his doctor with the feedback that could have saved his life.

Frequently, uncritical patients are lulled by doctors' reassurances, when, in fact, the doctors may be wrong. A woman with a lump in her breast repeatedly went to her doctor over a period of several months. Each time the doctor reassured her that she was all right. Because he was a well-known physician, the woman didn't think of going elsewhere. When at last the mass was biopsied, it turned out to be malignant. Nine months after the lump was first discovered, the woman's breast was removed. Because of her reverence for the doctor, she had endangered her life.

The medical mystique reveals itself today in the way physicians try to get you to comply with their instructions. Those of us doctors who act in a priestly way will beg, threaten, scold, frighten, and implore. Too rarely will we reason and reach the healthy feelings of the patient, and even more rarely will we want to be involved in a cooperative venture with the patient. But cajoling, scolding, frightening, and imploring, priestly mannerisms all, are not the best of behavioral or humanistic approaches, nor do they really work.

The last thing some doctors want is for you to question their diagnosis. If you question or doubt such physicians, they likely will reply, "Where did you get your degree?" or "Since when have you got a license to practice?" Some time ago a middle-aged man developed a lump underneath his jaw. His physician told him it was caused by an infection, and prescribed some medicine. The lump diminished in size, confirmation to the physician that his diagnosis had been correct. The lump did not disappear, and the patient worried. When he asked his doctor about it again, the doctor replied, "Are you the doctor?" So the patient did nothing further. But he was also concurrently in psychotherapy, and his therapist noticed the lump. He referred the patient to me. I found several other lumps, which were duly biopsied. It was Hodgkin's disease.

But the worst effects may be unrecorded. "Many people accept it as right and proper that patients should not understand the prescriptions their physicians hand them or that they should not know what is in their hospital records," Dr. Szasz observes. "At the same time they object to the indignities which the medical situation often imposes on them. The result of this ambivalence and inarticulated conflict is that people often feel anxious and humiliated at the prospect of seeking medical care and frequently avoid or reject such care altogether."

When patients don't want to present themselves to doctors at a time of illness, everyone is in trouble. The denial of illness is much more prevalent than hypochondriasis. Those who deny illness endanger their survival much more than those who exaggerate it.

Patients don't want to be labeled as hypochondriacs. How many times have you prefaced a recitation of symptoms to a doctor with the caution, "Now I don't want you to think I'm a hypochondriac . . ."? Or apologized for the "stupid" question you're about to ask. Or said, "Excuse me for bothering you." Or said, "Do you believe me?", as though the illness you've just described is one the doctor will think you've imagined. Patients actually apologize for their symptoms as though they are sinners who have committed some evil act. And most often, in such cases, they censor their list of symptoms. I know of one patient who visits his doctor only when he's in "tip-top" shape. If he's not feeling well, he won't come at all.

Men in their late forties and early fifties are particularly sensitive about being thought of as hypochondriacs. Many of them served in the Armed Forces in World War II, when a "goldbrick"—someone who often went on sick call—was considered a shirker. The pejorative stuck.

Patients will occasionally call to say that they can't come to the office because they're not feeling well. Of course they shouldn't come in if the trip is going to cause them pain, but too often that's not the case. What they are really saying is that they're ashamed to have the doctor see them in a state of illness, as though they've somehow disobeyed him, and he will disapprove.

Moreover, some patients come to the doctor in so humble a fashion, it is all but demeaning. The presumption is that you don't question the physician, any more than you question a deity.

HOW DOCTORS PERPETUATE THE MYSTIQUE

Both primitive and modern mystiques employ a jargon or lingo that separates "them" from the rest of us, and allows the mystery to be deepened. "They" become "high priests." Doctors use jargon today, both consciously and unconsciously; the effect is to reinforce the image of the expert and the inaccessibility of their thinking to the lay person.

For example, some doctors will talk to you about hypertension, on the assumption that you know what it means. But a recent survey reported that only twenty-four percent of the population understood the term, and that, of the people with hypertension, only thirty-three percent knew what it was. Many felt that it meant being high-strung, emotional or nervous. Hypertension is an arterial disease characterized by elevation of the blood pressure. Only thirteen percent of the total population and eighteen percent of the hypertensive population thought that high blood pressure was a major cause of heart trouble.

The priest always acted in an authoritative and authoritarian manner. Some physicians use such a manner just to promote their own importance.

A physician in New York City is known as a real showman; he dresses in stereotypic style, with vest and cravat and honorary pins dangling from a chain. His walls are covered with diplomas. His lectures to patients are stern, anguished, pontifical, and melodramatic. A doctor who practices in Chicago told me of a surgeon who has a terrible temper. He has tantrums in the operating room. He will throw instruments at a nurse, hurl his gloves to the floor, or stalk away from the table. His tantrums are tolerated because he is such a brilliant surgeon, but working with him is an ordeal that puts knots in his colleagues' stomachs. His tantrums detract from his abilities; his omniscience is a barrier between him and his patients.

Most doctors—thankfully—aren't nearly so colorful. For every example of a strutting or imperious or irascible doctor, I could give many examples of doctors whose dedication to their patients is manifested in the care they take in their diagnosis and treatment and the compassion they show in their attention and counsel. For instance, one doctor recovering in the hospital from a hernia operation was called and told that his patient was in the emergency room with severe chest pain. Despite some discomfort, he asked to be discharged so that he could care for the patient. Or: another doctor—when a taxi could not be flagged—pushed an elderly patient in a wheelchair to a medical center several blocks away to receive attention for a necessary diagnostic procedure.

But all doctors, good or bad, are human, a point that tends, not surprisingly, to elude their patients, and many doctors employ the medical mystique to barricade themselves from their patients. Perhaps they don't want any unnecessary intrusions on their busy schedules. If so, they present the image of a doctor in perpetual motion. The message is: don't bother the doctor with any irrelevancies, and the translation to the patient may be that his own problems are scarcely worthy of such an important man.

A University of Chicago researcher, Stephen Shortell, recently conducted a poll among doctors and patients to determine which kinds of physicians had the most prestige. The result: thoracic surgeons, neurosurgeons, and cardiologists. Analyzing the result, the study noted that the more active the doctor's role—the more he controlled outcome—the greater his prestige. Doctors involved in preventive medicine, allergy, and general practice were at the lower end of the ranking. Where the patient's role is a more active one, the doctor's prestige suffers which confirms again the prevalence of the mystique.

Some doctors are frightened, and assume an august position in order to exercise control over patients. Modern medicine can function as a panoply; just as the shamans set themselves into a mystical theater, using fires, totems, taboos, and sacrifices, so the modern doctor makes use of mysterious artifacts. He operates in an arena filled with lights and sound effects. He performs miracles with his instruments and magic potions.

Present-day technology so emphasizes mechanics and objects and creates such drama with them that we get the idea that technology itself can cure. Obviously, it can't. To the extent that this notion excludes other essentials of care, care itself is worsened.

In the times of the shaman, ritual determined who would approach him and how he would be addressed. The same tradition exists today. Some of it is helpful and necessary in order to assure optimum and orderly care. But some of it is window dressing. As the priestly class always had guards and servants to keep others from them, so many doctors today employ gatekeepers who mostly perform vital functions but occasionally act as though their most important duty is to keep the priest in his sanctuary, undisturbed by the supplicants.

I know of one doctor in Cleveland, very much a modern shaman, who is always late for appointments. He keeps his waiting room crowded with patients. He is a competent doctor, but he has an estimate of his abilities that would be hard for the best doctor in the world to fulfill. He needs to boast. He will buttonhole other doctors in a hospital corridor to tell them of "triumphs" that are routine and boring. He is condescending to the persons he's addressing. Behind their backs, he is hypercritical of other doctors' work and distorts what they have done. He will knock them needlessly in order to lift his own stature in the eyes of his patients. When he presents his findings to patients, he talks to them in a way that is incomprehensible and encourages them in the belief that only he could have diagnosed their illness. The pattern should be obvious to anyone with even the slightest familiarity with psychology. This doctor is almost totally lacking in self-confidence. He doesn't trust his knowledge.

Most of the doctors I know are men of goodwill. They have great warmth and compassion, and a high degree of skill. Often we fall short because of our lack of training—and occasionally our lack of interest—in educating and informing our patients.

THE RULES OF THE MYSTIQUE

Rules are necessary. They avoid chaos. But they must meet the test of usefulness, and they must not be used for the wrong purpose. They must constantly be reassessed in the light of changing conditions; if they have become obsolete, or serve as barriers to innovation made possible by new technology or changing attitudes, then they must be changed.

The medical mystique has its own rules and regulations. Many have compelling logic and are judiciously applied. But some of them ought to be questioned. The central question is whether the rules are used to promote the therapeutic aspects of the medical mystique, or whether they are employed to reinforce the mystique, or whether they are employed to reinforce the mystique's authoritarian aspects.

Hippocrates, in his oath, speaks not just of taking

care of patients, but of the obligations of all new members to their teachers. And fellows. Most lay people think of the Hippocratic oath as a dedication to the patient. But the oath also clearly defines what a doctor's obligations are to other members of the profession.

Two contemporary commentators on the medical profession, Henry F. Howe and Clyde T. Hardy, Jr., have described the general sets of rules that exist in the field of medicine. One physician must never publicly disparage another physician. No physician should publicly disparage the medical profession. The medical profession should protect the practitioner against public criticism. In *The Social System,* by Talcott Parsons, the author describes the efforts of organized medicine to make the patient cooperate—one might even say comply —with a physician. Patients who will not comply should be viewed as poor risks.

You are never supposed to go directly to a hospital or to another doctor. You are always referred by your own doctor. No doctor should interfere if you are another doctor's patient. A participant at one of my feedback sessions recounted an experience he'd had with his wife's obstetrician in a suburb in Boston. The obstetrician came down to the hospital waiting room to announce the birth of a son, and to invite the father upstairs to see his wife and child. They took an elevator to an upper floor—which rang with the screams of a woman in labor. They were the most terrifying screams the father had ever heard. The obstetrician paused at the frenzied woman's side. He looked at her chart, and hesitated, as though he ought to do something to help her. Then he turned to the father and said, "She's a patient of Doctor X. He's a good man. He knows what he's doing." Then the obstetrician moved on, leaving this young woman to suffer the pain of the moment and the possible psychological scars that she would carry with her through life.

Some doctors function on the assumption that you won't complain. That possibility doesn't even occur to them. The unspoken attitude they bring to the relationship is, "If you don't like me, get another doctor." They say, in effect, "Look, this is the kind of physician I am. This is the way I practice. Take it or leave it. It seems to work for the overwhelming majority of my patients, and it's not efficient or practical for me to change my style in order to accommodate you. It would take too much time, and it would detract from my work with my other patients. So take me as I am, or find another doctor."

The patient who is quite ill may give the doctor enough vital information for the doctor to make a proper diagnosis. Even if the patient doesn't complain, the doctor may find sufficient physical symptoms to locate the illness. But what is almost totally missing when a patient doesn't communicate is the kind of information that can locate the functional aspects of a disease. Diseases are not simply organic or structural. They express a patient's life.

It is artificial to separate diseases into organic or functional components, and equally artificial to separate a patient in the same manner. All organic diseases have functional and emotional components. Patients with heart disease or cancer or even infections such as a cold have accompanying emotional symptoms that very often influence and lessen resistance to such diseases. Emotions, in turn, can be the cause of functional symptoms.

In *Psychosomatic Medicine,* Dr. Ellie Henkle pointed out that there are periods of one's life when "clusters of illnesses" are associated with unsatisfactory and stressful events. Dr. R. H. Rahe, writing in the same journal five years later, noted that changes in an individual's accustomed way of life are significantly associated with the onset of illness. Such emotional causes of illness can never be perceived when the patient doesn't talk. Yet they permeate medicine, and keep people in an inferior state of health.

If the doctor were fulfilling his role as a medical teacher—providing the patients with clues to their illnesses—then you would have a greater awareness as to why, on many occasions, you don't feel well when you're not organically sick. You would describe symptoms to the doctor that may not reflect morbid pathology, but rather some underlying inability to adjust to stresses in the environment.

Instead, patients will complain of migraine headaches, but not the problems that are producing them. They won't acknowledge that they're unhappy at their jobs. They may be fearful of indicating to the physician that they're involved in sexual relationships outside their marriage that may be affecting their emotional health. Or they won't tell the physician the truth about how much they're drinking. Often they don't tell him because they feel he can somehow divine the problem. But most often the cause of their silence is their fear of being judged. They are afraid of the priest.

Sixty percent of all complaints by patients are rooted in functional causes. It is in this area where doctors are so helpless because patients can't articulate their problems. For this, blame the mystique.

HOW PATIENTS PERPETUATE
THE MYSTIQUE

Many of us need the godhead. We are happy with dependent relationships. It's as though we are grateful to be children once again.

Sickness and disability produce anxiety. When we are anxious we look to a deity or authority. Anxiety that reflects the reality of a patient's condition is a reliable index for the doctor, but when such anxiety is unduly heightened and exaggerated by the medical mystique, then it becomes deceptive and can send off misleading signals that can lead to diagnostic error.

We often accept relationships that should not be accepted. We tolerate care we should not tolerate. We say, "You're the doctor!" or, "Doctor knows best!" In doing this we are as much responsible for propagating the medical mystique as the physician.

Our expectations of the doctor often prevent the doctor from saying, "I don't know." We require an all-knowing oracle. Doctors, as a consequence, may attempt treatments for which they haven't sufficient skill or knowledge. They won't refer their patients to other specialists, when it's clearly in the patients' best interests to do so. They are constantly battling with the unconscious knowledge that they must maintain an all-knowing image or lose their patients' faith.

The world is full of dangers. You are liable to all kinds of stresses and attacks. Understandably, you look for reassurance, and outside help. The doctor is your most logical ally. Such interdependence is therapeutic. Many studies have demonstrated that when people are isolated they become demoralized and prone to disease. But there is a difference between dependency and interdependency. The child-like comfort obtained by abdicating responsibility for one's own welfare can be harmful.

To take away the mystique is to take away the

child in us. A new, more adult, aware and informed relationship with your physician will allow you to live more comfortably, and perhaps even longer.

The central problem of the medical mystique is whether you should abdicate your capacity for informed self-reliance and your powers of decision to the expert. We need the wisdom of experts. Experts, in turn, need the restraint of opinions. Detroit's experts can design ever more powerful automobiles. They need us to point out to them that such vehicles pollute the atmosphere and compound driving hazards.

Doctors and patients alike are creatures of an American idiom that validates bigness, newness, and absolutes. It is susceptible to fads and fashions. No wonder the medical mystique has flourished. With its capacity for cures and dramatic breakthroughs, it is culturally perfect.

But recent trends have enriched our culture and offer a healthy counter. The human potential movement tells us there is something special about our humanness—our ability to hope, aspire, struggle, change, and love. We have been reminded that individuality, self-reliance, activism, and the pioneering spirit are part of the American idiom too.

The consequences for medicine are marvelous to consider. They could mean an end to timidity, fear, confusion, inarticulateness, and ignorance among patients. They could mean an end to physicians who don't teach or explain, who don't inspire, guide, or care. They could mean a beginning of a truly helping participation between doctor and patient—with multitudes of lives enriched and extended.

2

How to Choose Your Doctor

DOCTORS DIFFER. The logic of that statement would seem obvious. Many patients understand this and choose their doctors accordingly. Most don't examine their physicians with sufficient care.

Is the doctor thorough or hurried? Is he up to date in his knowledge of medicines, diseases, and techniques or is he still practicing the medicine of the fifties? Are you the most important person in his life when you're talking to him, or does he seem distracted?

There are two things to look for in a doctor. The first is his competence. The second is his compassion. They are separate and yet indivisible. There is no competence without caring. The noncaring physician is a noncompetent physician. A doctor who won't hear what his patients have to say, who can't communicate ideas and inform, who can't express emotion and empathize with his patients, is an incompetent doctor.

Not long ago the daughter of a friend of mine was dying of leukemia. The mother was understandably overwrought and pressed the doctor with questions about what might be done to comfort her daughter. "What do you want? Somebody to hold her hand?" the doctor asked. "If that's the case, I suggest a minister or a psychiatrist—"

The woman studied the doctor for a moment and then replied, "I don't believe you're a doctor." He wasn't. He wasn't human, either. They go together.

The relationship between a patient and a doctor is a partnership. Just as you would want to know the personality, habits, and aspirations of any potential partner, so you need to know this doctor who is going to share your secrets, probe your body, and perhaps one day hold your life in his hands. To acquire such knowledge you must learn to be sufficiently assertive in a society that teaches people to revere authority. You must be every bit as vigorous and forthright as you would be in a successful marriage.

Not only do you have the right to judge your physician, you have a responsibility to judge him. And your physician should welcome this as a way of improving the kind of care he can render. The critical evaluation of his work and how he relates to you should continue throughout your relationship.

Your first task in this partnership is to choose the right *kind* of physician.

"A bewildering variety of medical specialists now minister to each corner of the human body and psyche," *Consumer Reports* once noted in the preface to an article on "How to Find a Doctor for Yourself." "But the primary need is for a personal physician for yourself and your family."

The primary-care physician you're looking for is either an internist or a family practitioner.

I'm an internist. I diagnose and treat internal diseases. I see some patients for health maintenance and disease prevention; I see others who have chronic diseases, or continuing problems, such as cardiopulmonary disease, gastrointestinal disease, kidney disease, arthritis, diabetes. I also think of myself as a practicing family physician concerned with my patients' overall lives.

The general practitioner, or GP, was once the primary-care physician for most people; he began to practice as soon as he finished his internship. Today, doctors who intend to become family practitioners take additional training in such areas as preventive medicine, internal medicine, minor surgery, orthopedics, gynecology, and pediatrics. And like internists they may also study the science of human behavior, which wasn't the case in the time of the old general practitioner.

It's important for all primary-care physicians to treat the entire family. They can relate the illness of one of its members to what's occurring within the family. It's not just a matter of disease being transmitted from one member to another; it's a matter of the social or emotional or economic climate within the family that may be contributing to illness. Family practitioners and internists are concerned with how patients behave toward other members of their family. They want to know what life is like at home, what jobs the various members hold, how the children are doing at school, how well the parents get along.

The difference between an internist and a family practitioner is a matter of training, and specialties. An internist, for example, doesn't normally take training in pediatrics, orthopedics or child delivery. On the other hand, he will know more than the family practitioner about the heart, lungs, kidney, gastrointestinal system, liver, endocrine system, and diseases such as arthritis.

A good primary-care physician doesn't abandon you to a specialist or fragment your care. He does refer you if you have special, unusual problems beyond his ability, or if you simply want another medical opinion. He functions here as the integrator and synthesizer in the team concept of medical care. He will know when the time has come to refer you to a specialist.

But the optimum kind of care is the one in which

the doctor knows you as a human being, knows your family, knows the influences on your life that might be affecting your health. Too often, some specialists' thinking is highly focused on their own fields of expertise. Patients with pain in their backs may go directly to an orthopedist. Unfortunately, some orthopedists may look at them only as patients with back problems and will not have a complete picture of their medical condition. And the patient rarely will give the specialist all information that would relate his other problems to his back problem. I knew a woman with a backache who had gone directly to an orthopedist. He couldn't find the cause. Eventually, her primary-care physician discovered that she had been having sexual problems with her husband; her inability to have an orgasm was producing a pelvic congestion syndrome.

Patients today are too prone to fragment their care. They want a stomach doctor, a heart doctor, a kidney doctor. Too often they want a "big man"—not because they have evaluated his competence but because of his reputation and the status it conveys. It is part of our American idiom to admire greatness. And greatness in our culture tends to mean bigness. But greatness or bigness has nothing necessarily to do with being good. There *are* good doctors and bad doctors. The route to the so-called big man is often not the best one to choosing a physician. A physician's place on a social pedestal doesn't equate with competence. Your doctor shouldn't be a status symbol for you; too often and for too many he is.

It's in your own interest not to fragment your care by going to an orthopedist, allergist, or other specialist *at the outset*. If you have a problem of unknown origin, the best rule is to begin with your family practitioner or internist and then move on to the specialist if the situation warrants; in such cases the primary-care physician can help determine the degree of specialization required, select a qualified specialist, and serve as your advocate during treatment.

The primary-care doctor usually has the benefit of a long association with you. He will, for example, be aware of any emotional situation which could affect the treatment of a disease such as asthma or hypertension. And because of his long relationship with you, the primary-care physician is likely to be more involved with you. He will be more apt to see you as a person instead of a problem. He will know at least something of your emotional background.

The specialist *should* show the same compassion as the primary-care physician; compassion is an essential ingredient of competent care, communication, and healing. And many fine specialists do show concern. But like most human beings, they are bound to feel more for persons they know well —and because of the nature of their work they don't commonly form long relationships with patients.

Patients who would never accept a lack of compassion on the part of their primary-care physician tend to accept a cold, one-shot encounter with a specialist. You should expect the same compassion from both; you won't get it until you do.

PREVISIT STRATEGY

Let's assume you're starting fresh. You haven't got a regular doctor, and you'd like to find one. Or you're dissatisfied with your present doctor and would like to find a new one. How do you go about it? Is there any way you can judge a doctor's competence before you actually see him? Obviously you can't do so fully. But you can make some intelligent estimates.

First, compile a list of names. The most common way to do that is to consult with relatives and friends, but it can be the least reliable, especially if not followed by your own close personal evaluation.

There are other resources. Every local medical society has a medical referral bureau that will provide you with a membership list of licensed doctors; the same list is probably available in your local library. Neither the society nor its list will tell you anything about the competence of the doctors, how they compare with one another, or how much they charge. But you'll be able to put together a select list of doctors by specialty and location.

Other sources for lists are the teaching hospital nearest you or a medical school in your area. The hospital should be able to give you a list of internists or family practitioners who are on its staff. Members of the medical school's faculty will often have private practices.

A public-interest group in your community may have developed a list of the community's physicians. The first such attempt to compile one was made in Prince Georges County, Maryland, in 1973 by Ralph Nader's Health Research Group. This survey produced a list of more than one hundred physicians, with information about the doctors' schedules, fees, availability, the nature of their practices and office personnel, the time allotted per patient, their hospital affiliations, and even their competence in foreign languages. By 1974, consumer organizations in thirty-two other states were reportedly preparing their own consumers' guides to doctors.

The most obvious item on such a list is the doctor's fee. A doctor who refuses to discuss his fee is exhibiting the medical mystique at its worst. And a high fee does not necessarily mean superb care.

Many elements go into determining a physician's fee: his training and experience, the town in which he works and lives, and, most important, the time he spends on your problems—not only in a face-to-face encounter but in making and evaluating tests and in consulting with other physicians. The time given to you by his medical assistants may be another factor. The use to which his office equipment is put in your behalf is another. There may be special circumstances associated with a particular illness that require extra attention or additional technology. All of these are fair considerations.

At the outset, of course, you can't know how most of these variables affect you. Right now your basic task is to find out the charges for a regular office visit, and a call to the doctor's office requesting this information is absolutely in order. You then need to consider whether you are comfortable with the doctor's fee, or if its size will adversely affect your relationship.

You should also check out a doctor's hospital further on, but for now it's important to remember that a *teaching* hospital—one that is part of, or affiliated with, a medical school—has much to commend it. Dr. John H. Knowles put it well in *Scientific American:* "The best medical care is achieved in this environment of constant inquiry and scrutiny by a number of people (medical students, house staff interns and residents, senior staff professionals and practicing physicians) where scientific and technological knowledge can be applied within the shortest period of time after its development."

Formal training is a third vital element for

you to consider. Which medical school did he graduate from? Which hospital did he serve in as an intern and resident? What specialty training has he had in the years since? During the post-graduate years a physician will undergo rigorous training in the area of his specialization. At this time his skills and acumen are sharpened under the supervision of knowledgeable specialists. In judging the training and background of your physician, keep in mind especially that the best primary-care and specialist training take place in a hospital affiliated with a university medical school.

THE MEDICAL-SCHOOL MYSTIQUE

Generally, the quality of a medical school is akin to the quality of the undergraduate school with which it is affiliated. But because a doctor has not been trained at one of the so-called "big" schools does not mean he hasn't received competent training. American medical schools, generally, achieve a high degree of excellence.

The earliest medical schools were proprietary, set up mainly for profit. Anyone could get in. The teaching was mediocre, at best; often, it was abysmal. At the beginning of the twentieth century most of these schools were shut down. They were replaced by university-affiliated medical schools, which served as models for many others and tended to be research-oriented.

But the kinds of rare diseases that make fascinating research are rarely seen in medical practice. And today many medical schools have begun to emphasize community medicine. Medical schools, generally, could benefit from even more courses in patient education, communication skills, humanistic psychology, patient motivation, and patient-doctor feedback techniques.

Doctors, of course, should be judged not only on their training but on how well they've put it to practice: How do they relate to people? Do they take an adequate history? Do they interview well? How intensively do they examine? Do they make proper use of laboratory facilities? How well do they diagnose and supervise continuing care? Do they have good hospital affiliations? In short, they should be judged as doctors and not by labels.

The same applies to graduates of foreign medical schools.

Many people are suspicious of American doctors trained in foreign schools. Some of these doctors, obviously, did not compare favorably to other students who applied, at the same time, for places in U.S. medical schools. And, upon being turned down in the United States, they enrolled in foreign schools. The training in these foreign schools may not be as desirable, thorough, or technologically competent as training in U.S. medical schools, yet many doctors who graduate from such schools may be every bit as good as other doctors with more expert training. Their enthusiasm for practicing medicine helped them persevere to a point where they finally gained their training. And with proper postgraduate training, many have become fine physicians. It is important, therefore, to find out the kind of training a foreign-schooled physician received *after* medical school.

When and if my son goes into medicine, however, I would prefer that he go to an institution in this country. I do believe there's a qualitative difference between university-affiliated medical schools in this country and most foreign medical schools—a minority of foreign medical-school graduates, thirty to forty percent, pass the initial qualifying examinations that permit them to practice medicine in this country.

WHAT THE DEGREE DOESN'T TELL YOU

Lists and surveys, however compiled, are only starting points. They can help you find a doctor, but they can't help you judge him. It's really not enough to know what training he received. You must also know something about the forces at work on his personality.

Most young people who become physicians know rather early in life that they want careers in medicine. And most of them are highly motivated. They perceive medicine as a way to help people. I remember how disturbed I was as a young boy because my paternal grandparents were always sick. I often wondered if something could be done for them that wasn't being done. It was irrational for the world to be so full of sickness. By going into medicine, I could help understand sickness— and do something to change what was wrong.

But there were other, more complex motivations for me, and I think for most doctors. As a child I recall having fears of dying. My mother had arthritis and had to go to doctors frequently. Occasionally I went with her. The visits to the doctor somehow reassured me. It was as though this gentle, soft-spoken man had the knowledge, instruments, and potions to defeat death.

My father, unlike my mother, had critical feelings about doctors. He didn't like show or artifice in anyone, and he would object if anyone attempted to put people on pedestals. My questioning attitude may very well have originated with my father. And yet those reassuring visits to the doctor with my mother left their imprint as well.

I mention these personal matters simply to emphasize that doctors begin their studies as young men and women with histories, associations, and motivations. Their motivations are generally high but there are cases where their reasons for going into medicine may not necessarily be consistent with your interests and needs.

A desire to be powerful or omnipotent or the center of attention, a neurotic fascination with illness and death, an attraction to the trappings of medicine—none of these is sound motivation for a career in medicine. Yet there are men and women who have sought, and do seek, medical careers for such reasons.

Doctors are also not immune to American cultural values. Some may be motivated primarily to make a comfortable living. Our culture has been accused of emphasizing things more than people. To the extent that the charge has validity, doctors are as susceptible as any other group. Early training, moreover, can reinforce such values. Medicine sometimes begins with things and objects, not people.

THE DETACHMENT OF YOUNG DOCTORS

When people say, "My doctor doesn't talk to me," that's not what it started out to be. Something happens along the way. The mechanized activity of early training in medical school can desensitize some medical students to the human aspects of care.

To understand your doctor better, you will be helped by knowing what kind of training he went through, and how he reacted to it.

Medical school is an experience in isolation. It may often breed insularity. The concerns of a medical student are so highly technical that they spill over into other parts of his life. His focus and leisure time may become relatively narrow. He submits to a process that may turn him into less a person than an object to be filled with knowledge and passed on. Only occasionally is he given an opportunity to explore the emotions and feelings aroused by this experience at medical school. He rarely, if ever, discusses with his teachers or fellow students what it means to see death, or to have to make decisions that could affect life, or to make a critical mistake. He erects psychological armor.

The young medical student works first not with a living, breathing human, but with a cadaver. Every doctor can tell you about the impact of this experience. The sight of a black leather shroud over a human form is jarring. The shroud remains in place as you begin to work. You start with a hand, lifeless, of course. Once the first cut is made, the hand loses all semblance of what it is, and becomes, instead, a collection of tendons, nerves, and arteries.

Here begins the process of detachment. The hand as an object becomes a defense mechanism for the future doctor. It's one way that he or she can control the attending emotions. The body must lose its history as a person. One day, much later, the doctor may begin to view patients as objects, too, in order to protect himself from feelings.

If a physician is not in touch with his own feelings, it will be difficult for him to comprehend the feelings of his patients. And the blame for such detachment must be placed, in large part, on the mechanized training he receives in medical school. This training can desensitize some students to the human aspects of care.

It is not a process that occurs inevitably, nor is it necessarily continuous. It flares up and remits, like a disease. And it works differently on different students.

I shall never forget one episode from my student days. I was following an obstetrical resident on hospital rounds, and he approached the bed of a woman who was giving an intern difficulties. She was pregnant and about to deliver, but she refused to be examined. The woman was on a drug called scopolamine, which was supposed to sedate her but which also tended to make her hyperactive and untrusting. Now the woman was screaming at the doctor to leave her alone. The resident pinned the woman to the corner of the bed, instructed others to hold her legs, and performed the internal examination. It was important for him to know how far in labor she had gone, but I thought then—and think now—that there must be a better way.

A compassionate doctor would have tried to find

out why the woman was terrified. He would have encouraged her to talk about her feelings, and indicated he understood why she was so afraid. He would have attempted to comfort her. If necessary, he would have obtained someone whom she trusted to be with her. Such efforts might not have totally persuaded the woman to be examined, but they would have helped.

When people are ill, it's obviously important to examine them, but sometimes the examination itself causes additional discomforts. The patient's feelings may date back to when he or she had an injection as a child. But the feeling is real and must be considered. It's got to be accepted that in the uncovering of illness there is pain and suffering—a subject that should be more adequately covered in medical school.

And yet all medical students undergo the inevitable compensating experience of meeting with their first patient. My own experience did much to restore the balance.

She was an elderly woman, deeply jaundiced. I remember thinking, "Oh, my God, is she sick!" She was also frightened and lonely. It was my job to examine her and then report my findings to my teachers. It was unlikely I was going to learn anything about her that someone with more training hadn't already learned. There was little chance that I, with the limited knowledge of a medical student, was going to discover some bright new therapeutic direction. In fact, the poor woman was dying. And yet she greeted me with such regard, as though I were coming to her with a truly special skill. No matter who examined her, she always had a bit of hope that maybe this person, even a student, might find something that would save her.

There was little I felt I could really do for her. And yet apparently my concern so comforted her that it actually made a difference. She became more ambulatory. She ate better. She felt stronger. For me, the experience pierced the psychological armor I'd built up against the fears and uncertainties of medical school. It reminded me why I had wanted to become a doctor.

IS YOUR DOCTOR INTERESTED IN YOU—OR YOUR CASE?

There are patients from whom doctors can't learn. They aren't professionally "stimulating." They are just plain sick. The classification of patients into those who are professionally "rewarding" and those who aren't is one of the unfortunate hangovers of medical education. If the doctor you're considering finds you medically dull, pass to another doctor.

On the other hand, if you're one of those patients who has a disease that doctors find professionally stimulating, be careful, too. Because sometimes the disease becomes more significant than you. When this happens, you'll know it.

I once had a patient who disliked visiting my office. I could never understand why. One day, finally, I told her that her attitude puzzled me and asked her to explain. "It's got nothing to do with you," she began. And then she recounted as a distressing story about doctors as I've heard.

She was born with a defective heart. There is a little duct that shunts the embryo's blood from one side of the heart to the other. When the baby is born, the lungs immediately expand and the blood then passes through them. The shunt, no longer necessary, is closed by pressure from the lungs. In this woman's case, the shunt hadn't closed. The condition is known as patent ductus arteriosis. It requires the heart to work doubly hard to pump blood into the lungs because so much of it continues to pass through the duct.

When the woman was a child, there was no surgical process to remedy the defect. She had lived a special, protected life, unable to do anything that would be strenuous. Her parents took her to many doctors, and each time she went she sensed that the doctors were interested not in her but in her special heart. In hospitals, the doctors would all flock to her bedside; all of them wanted to examine her. Shortly after her marriage to a man in military service she went into an army hospital to find out if it would be safe for her to have children. It happened again—the young service doctors flocked to her bedside to learn from this fascinating *case*. By now there was a surgical process to sever the duct and tie it off. Several days after the young woman entered the hospital, the doctors solemnly gathered *around her husband* at the foot of her bed, and recommended surgery. She was literally forgotten. The husband favored the surgery; she agreed to have it but not in that setting. Fortunately, a year later she found a surgeon who treated her like a person, not a defective heart. He performed the surgery, and she is now in her forties, with a healthy heart.

There are, of course, some patients who thrive on being "interesting" cases because of the attention it gets them. They may even exaggerate their symptoms. But others can be frightened by the overzealousness of the doctors. One of my patients, an elderly woman, went into the hospital for complicated surgery. Afterward several doctors gathered around her bed to make sure she received a certain type of intravenous treatment at a certain prescribed rate. It had to be particularly aseptic. The woman heard their conversation and became so frightened that she trusted no one. She began to watch nothing but the bottle above her bed; anyone who came near it was out to do her harm. Worse, she began to despair of ever getting well.

The need to have clinical conversations is unquestioned, but the brilliance of these physicians did not have to be demonstrated in front of the poor woman's bedside. The moral of the story for anyone choosing a physician is that technological competence simply isn't enough. Physicians have a healing function as well, which they must exercise whether you are a "crock"—doctors' parlance for the uninteresting patient—or a patient with a unique illness.

The doctor's degree is not meaningful until you determine how his medical school experience affected him. If all you want is a technician, then it's textbook competence you're after. But the art of healing involves more than textbooks. It involves a relationship between you and your doctor that will engage and tax both of you. Your reaction to your physician *as a person* is really the most important consideration in your choice of a doctor.

You have to decide whether the doctor is the kind of person you're willing to confide in. Remember that at least sixty percent of the problems you bring to him will have emotional antecedents.

When I went to medical school more than twenty years ago, we were taught that we should give comfort to the patients. Fine, but we received little training in *how* to provide comfort. Our training was mostly technological. But healing also involves the emotional process. Every disease comes freighted with emotion. Then, as now, the disease was dealt with but often the emotion was set aside, or assigned to another doctor's province.

Academic excellence rather than a compassionate makeup is the prime criterion for acceptance into medical school. But to change a patient from one condition to another condition—which is what physicians do—is going to change the patient emotionally as well as biologically. When you give a patient digitalis, a drug to correct heart failure, and in the process save his life, you have most certainly changed that patient as a person. Most doctors can correctly prescribe digitalis, but only some will, or know how to, deal with the new person who emerges from the experience.

Some doctors may argue that emotional response to illness isn't their domain. They don't even have time to treat thoroughly the psychological consequences of illness, and/or they don't have the knowledge—that's for the psychiatrist. If your doctor makes this argument, or if his treatment of you and your family has not involved attention to the emotional aspects of your situation, you might consider looking for another doctor. The psychological dimension can't be divorced in any way from any medical practice. The physician who divorces it just isn't meeting his responsibilities.

Nor is the doctor who moves patients along on a beltline, giving a shot here and a prescription there. He needs to understand that if a patient develops heart failure prematurely, it may be because somewhere along the line he, the doctor, was unable to motivate the patient to reduce his salt intake—or because the patient wasn't, for example, able to cope with denial, or anger about being sick.

The average doctor, it's true, does not deal with psychiatric patients. He deals with normal people who may have psychological problems that accompany illness. Those problems need to be dealt with by the physician-patient team. You need to choose a doctor, if possible, who believes in this.

CLUES TO THE DOCTOR'S BEHAVIOR

You've considered your friends' recommendations, consulted the directory of physicians in your local library, or called the local hospital or medical school and asked for a list of doctors. You've learned what you can about the doctor of your choice: his education, special training, hospital affiliation, the nature of his practice, his hours, location, and fees. To this factual information, you've added the impressions of others who might know the doctor firsthand. The last step is to assess the doctor personally (keeping in mind, hopefully, some of the thoughts in the immediately preceding pages). You want to see for yourself how he functions. There is no way to assess the doctor's human qualities and values except by a visit in which you examine and interact with him.

How do you make this assessment?

Whether or not you have any special or scientific knowledge, there are certain clues in your doctor's behavior, the content of his discussions with you and the environment he works in.

You'll want to make sure, right off, that he is oriented toward preventive medicine and health maintenance. There is no better indication of that than his own person. He should present himself as a health model, motivating his patients by example.

If you have a perennial weight problem, there's probably a better choice for you than a fat physician. And if you're a smoker and think you should probably give it up, a doctor who smokes won't be much inspiration. It's tragic that anyone smokes; it's especially tragic when a doctor smokes.

The doctor's appearance tends to project his own estimate of his value as a person. This has nothing to do with style or modishness. His orderliness or lack of it tells you whether or not he respects himself. His girth and bearing, the clarity of his eyes, tell you whether or not he cares for his body by exercising. Is he alert? Or does he appear sleepy or tired? It may be you're catching him after an early-morning emergency. But the doctor who is in good physical condition can rebound from such an experience. Maybe something has happened in his personal life that's made him fatigued and sloppy. In any case, it's still a distraction that can affect the care he will give you.

You shouldn't, of course, expect your doctor to be godlike or perfect. The whole point of your new relationship is to understand that he's a human being, like you, with the same kinds of problems you have. But he has an added responsibility to you that obliges him to live up to certain standards. If in the course of your relationship he begins to drink heavily, it will show in the energy and alertness he brings to your care.

His waiting room is also an indication of his attitude toward his patients. It doesn't have to be expensive to be attractive. It should be a warm office, a bright office, an office that's clean and is kept that way. Too often doctors' offices have a clinical look about them. That isn't necessary. There's a way to make a doctor's waiting room look as inviting as a living room. That's not pretension on the doctor's part; to the contrary, a skillfully decorated office can do much to relieve your anxieties. Such an office can help you feel that the circumstances you're in aren't so terrifyingly different from normal.

If the office is messy, crowded, dingy, you're probably not in the right office. It's likely another manifestation of the medical mystique—the doctor feels he's so important that the setting he functions in doesn't matter. Patients who accept such conditions are perpetuating the mystique and taking a needless risk.

Background: Doctors differ ethically and philosophically. Their attitudes on drinking or sex may reflect the cultures they come from. The doctor who was raised puritanically may not be able to discuss your sexual problems with you as comfortably as one who was raised in a less restrictive culture. Some doctors on religious grounds may, understandably, have difficulty in recommending an abortion. I make a point of giving my pertinent background information to any patient. If it makes a difference to them, they can ask for another recommendation.

The doctor's sex is another obvious consideration. If you're a woman, would you be more comfortable with a female gynecologist? If you're a man, would you be comfortable with a woman physician? Ideally, the doctor's sex shouldn't make a difference, but if *you* feel it's going to make a difference, it's important for you to deal with that feeling.

The increasing presence of women in the medical profession is long overdue. By almost any yardstick, American medicine has shown a consistent bias against women. Only nine percent of American doctors are women compared to twenty-four percent in Great Britain and sixty-five percent in the Soviet Union. Whatever other factors may account for this disproportion, one factor has surely been male chauvinism. A seven-year study of medical schools and their administrators by Dr. Harold I. Kaplan, a psychiatrist at New York Medical College, uncovered a widely held view that women were emotionally unsuited to be doctors. (Grammar, incidentally, not male chauvinism, dictates the use of the masculine pronoun in this book; it should be understood that the word "doctor" throughout refers to both men and women.)

The doctor's age needs to be frankly considered, too. It may seem an older doctor would have more experience whereas the younger doctor would be equipped with all the latest medical armament. But it's not quite that simple. It isn't true that because a doctor is old he's necessarily dated. A good doctor *always* tries to grow and mature and adopt the best and latest. Creativity, innovation, a capacity for change, the energy to stay current, the ability and willingness to relate to younger colleagues who can help him keep abreast of developments—all of these characterize the young doctor of any age. As in most professions, there are "old" young men and "young" old men. Don't go by the date on the diploma hanging on the wall. Go by the person.

THE ENCOUNTER

Before you step through that door, you should have some expectations pretty firmly in mind.

You have a right to be fully informed; you should learn from your doctor anything he learns about you. This information should be given to you in a manner and with a vocabulary that you can understand, without jargon or lingo.

You have a right to the doctor's time. He should be available and accessible to you. If for some reason he can't be, he should arrange for a suitable substitute.

You have a right to the doctor's continuing professional competence.

You have a right to be treated with compassion.

You have a right to confidentiality.

You have a right to know everything about a physician that is relevant to your treatment.

You have a right to be educated.

You have a right to question the doctor, to make suggestions, and be critical when appropriate.

If you leave your doctor, you have a right to have your records sent to a doctor of your choice.

The most important factor in judging a new doctor—or in reappraising your present doctor—is *time*. The doctor's thoroughness will be evident in his manner, his procedure, and his physical examinations.

Does he give you his undivided attention? Does he allow frequent interruptions? Does he welcome your questions? Does he seem relaxed? Or does he appear rushed, and does he rush you?

Does he give you a feeling that you're intruding on his time?

He should give you a feeling of calm and assurance. This isn't to say that at times he won't show frustration or anger. He's just as human as you are. But such displays should be appropriate to the circumstances. If he told you after your heart attack to eliminate salt from your diet and learns now that you haven't done so, some show of frustration or anger or both is appropriate and probably to your benefit—the lack of it *might* even suggest indifference.

The dominant consideration, though, should be his warmth and compassion for you.

It's also important for a physician to be able to say he's sorry. He should be able to say, "I've made a mistake."

He should be concerned about the kind of work you do, the kind of problems you have in your family. Such matters should be discussed on your very first visit.

He should know you at the end of the first visit well enough to help you. That means he must know about your sex life, the kind of food you eat, the amount of exercise you do, the way you sleep.

One of his questions should be "Are you happy?" or something to this effect. He should want to know about your goals. He should also be specifically interested in how your current illness has affected you emotionally, how it's affected your life.

Here's a small list of questions I regularly ask my patients:

> Do you feel frustrated about anything?
> Are you drinking more than you used to?
> Is anything bothering you at home?
> Are you happy with the way your children
>   turned out?
> Are you satisfied with your job?
> Do you have an adequate sex life?

All of these questions should be asked whether or not you have given your doctor any clues about whether you're bothered in any of these areas. Your doctor should want to know a great deal more than you expect to tell him. If you feel you're telling him things about your life that you hadn't expected to share, you're probably in the company of a caring physician.

It's absolutely vital to your survival that you and your physician open yourselves up to direct, honest communication. You're endangered if you don't, much like the woman who came to me with a complaint that she was feeling tired and had no appetite. When I took a history I asked her if she'd ever used drugs. She said no. I suspected otherwise and that she'd contracted hepatitis. When I looked at her arms I found no incriminating marks. Then I asked her to undress so I could examine her. She refused. But by blood chemistries I found that she did have serum hepatitis, and that it was drug-induced. Later

I learned that she'd been doing some injecting in an area close to her rectum. But she couldn't breach that last gap of trust and confidence and confide her embarrassing secret—even though it was vital knowledge I needed to help her recover.

I've had patients with alcohol on their breath insist to me that they hadn't been drinking—elevated blood alcohols confirmed they had.

These kinds of encounters have made me painfully aware of the dangerous lack of doctor-patient communication.

Finally, although some may tend to overlook it, the most important consideration in assessing your doctor is whether he makes you well.

THE EXAMINATION

A doctor should take a complete history on your first visit. Many don't. A doctor can't practice quality care if he doesn't take a full history because the presenting symptom—the problem that brought you to the doctor's office—has many antecedents. A patient's palpitations today may be related to the fact that he had rheumatic fever as a child. And a doctor requires this knowledge in order to evaluate the current problem. But a patient often does not volunteer the necessary information about his past. He'll only tell what's bothering him now. He should be made aware by his doctor that there's a possible link between his current palpitations and a disease he had forty or fifty years ago.

As part of the history, the physician should take a "review of systems"—a series of questions about all the body's organs and related symptoms.

PREVIOUS MEDICAL HISTORY

Family history
Illnesses
Hospitalizations
Allergies
Accidents
Previous surgery

REVIEW OF SYSTEMS

Neuromuscular
  Any fainting spells?
  Any dizzy spells?
  Headaches?
  Can you see well?
  Any spots or flashes before the eyes?
  Any difficulty in hearing?
  Any ringing in the ears?
  Any double vision?
  Any weakness, numbness or tingling in the
      extremities?
  Any trouble walking?
  Any muscle tenderness or pain?

Gastrointestinal

Any change in weight?

How's your appetite?

Are your bowels regular?

Any change in bowel pattern? Diarrhea? Constipation?

Any blood in the stool? Any change in color of stool?

Any indigestion? Does food bother you? Any particular foods?

Any abdominal pain?

Any nausea or vomiting?

Any trouble swallowing?

Any heartburn?

Any gas?

Genitourinary

Any burning on urination?

Any blood in urine?

Do you wake up to urinate at night?

Do you urinate often?

Do you urinate a great deal at any one time?

Any trouble starting the stream?

Any sense of urgency?

Has the color of your urine changed?

(Men)

Any difficulty with erection?

Any change in sexual habits or desire?

(Women)

Are periods regular? Excessive? Too little?

Any bleeding between periods?

Any pain with period?

Any pain with intercourse?

Any vaginal discharge?
Are you using a contraceptive?
If you've had a pregnancy, how did it go?
Any change in sexual habits or desire?

Respiratory

Do you produce mucus?
Any coughing?
Any shortness of breath?
Sore throats?
Any hoarseness?
Any wheezing?
Do you ever cough up blood? When? Where? How much?
Any nosebleeds? What duration?
Any earaches? Any discharge from the ears?
Any feelings of congestion?
Any sweating, particularly night sweating?
Any chest discomfort or pain? If so, is it relieved by rest?

Cardiovascular

Any chest pain? Feeling of pressure? Discomfort?
Any palpitation? Fluttering? Any feeling that you've skipped a beat?
Any history of murmur?
Any ankle swelling?
Any excessive or quick weight gain?
Any weakness?
Any pains in leg muscles? Other muscles?
Any pain when walking? Do you get relief with rest?

Skin
    Any itching?
    Any eruptions?
    Any sores or lumps?
    Any change in the color of your skin?
    Lighter? Darker?
    Any rash?
    Any spontaneous black-and-blue marks?

Joints (fingers, wrists, elbows, shoulders,
    hips, back, ankles, toes)
    Any pain or swelling?
    Any redness?
    Any inflammation?
    Any stiffness?
    Any discomfort or ache, particularly in the
    back?

PERSONAL HISTORY

Age
Sex
Ethnic background
Job situation (any exposure to fumes, chemi-
    cals)
Health habits
    Do you drink alcohol?
    Do you drink coffee?
    Do you smoke?
    Do you take drugs?
    How do you sleep, and for how many
    hours?
    What sort of sex life do you have?

Family milieu
   Nutrition
   Leisure-time pursuits
   Travel
   Exercise

As you talk to the doctor, note how much he's writing down. Records that list a symptom but don't describe it in some detail aren't very useful. For example, suppose the doctor writes down "coughed up blood." That's not enough. It's important to know whether the color of the blood was bright or dark, how long the blood had been present, whether there was any chest pain associated with the coughing, whether there had been any previous episodes and whether any X-rays had ever been taken in connection with these complaints. Your doctor should also note all this down because you may change doctors one day and want to take your records with you.

The same meticulous, searching approach should be used in the physical examination. And—this is important though it may seem self-evident—you should be asked to undress so you can be fully examined.

The physician has access to the innermost secrets of the patient, and the most private parts of his body. There can be no secrets and no shields if the patient is to receive helping care. But the doctor should understand that this privilege granted to him by a patient is a gift of trust; it must be respected.

His examination should be done with dignity and humanity. It should be undertaken with the greatest respect one individual can show for another.

There's nothing complex about judging your doctor's concern. You know when you're being treated with dignity by another human being. That's the measure you apply to your doctor.

As you're being examined, you should be aware of how your doctor uses laboratory tools and data. A well-equipped doctor's office today has an X-ray machine (primarily for chest X-rays), cardiographic tools, and a laboratory to test blood count, urine and blood chemistries. If your doctor doesn't have the facilities to check you out thoroughly, he should send you to a laboratory for this work.

Obviously it's better for you if the work can be handled in his office in one visit. It's more convenient and efficient. He may even have some of the results while you're with him. He can interpret the findings for you and immediately impress on you what you should do in the light of those findings.

A doctor's competence is measured by how well he utilizes and evaluates laboratory data every bit as much as by how well he takes a history and performs a physical examination. So your evaluation of the doctor depends on your ability to assess his competence in these matters as well. To help you, in chapter 4, we'll examine in detail how a doctor makes a diagnosis.

For now, please keep in mind that tests, like

clinical impressions, may be tentative and may require repetition. This shouldn't cause alarm. One test doesn't make a diagnosis. Abnormal results always need to be retested and reconfirmed.

A good doctor, a "young" doctor, as we've suggested, will give you the feeling that he's someone who's interested in change. He keeps up. He reads regularly in the medical journals. He attends medical conventions. You have a right to ask him how he keeps up with the latest innovations.

One specific way to find out is to determine whether the doctor has been certified by the American Medical Association for having continued his medical education. New programs of continuing education have recently become available to physicians. Ask your doctor if he involves himself in such programs.

If you haven't found out about the doctor's hospital affiliation, now is the time. Remember, again, that the best hospital is one affiliated with a medical school. And in a place where no medical school is nearby, a good community hospital will try to shape its program with a feeling for teaching and continuing postgraduate education. Try to find a doctor who is on its staff.

Obviously, you can find a poor physician in a good hospital, and vice versa, but it's better to have a good physician in a good hospital. Once you know your doctor is in such a hospital, at least you know that you have an optimal combination for good treatment. If you're ever critically ill it's comforting to know that you're going to be receiving the best in nursing care, intern and resident supervision, and laboratory expertise.

Your previsit research presumably gave you the information you needed about your doctor's fee schedule. If not, now is the time to discuss it. Patients don't generally like to talk about fees. Neither do doctors. If nobody talks about fees, the result can be needless antagonism later on.

MAKING YOUR DIAGNOSIS

You're not going to know everything about your doctor after one visit any more than he'll know everything about you. But there are certain minimal things you can know that can give clues about what your relationship might be like.

If any doctor assumes a role that is lordly, or patronizing, or even paternal, this doctor will have many distortions in his relationship with you. He should not be mechanistic or cold. He should emphasize hope and comfort. He should make you feel as optimistic as possible, consistent with the facts and conclusions about your illness.

You should never feel that you are being controlled by the doctor, that you have to follow blindly without indicating to him, look, this is the way I see it, this is what I can do, this is my feeling about how you act toward me.

The doctor you want is someone who likes to have an active, participating patient. He doesn't have all the answers. He knows he can get many of the answers from his patient.

The more you know about your body, the better it is for your doctor. Some doctors may resent the knowledge you've picked up through the media and popular reading. I think it's all to the good that such information be openly discussed. Those doctors who resent your knowledge may look on it as a threat to their authoritarian role. But a good physician is someone who encourages your involvement in the health world. With one obvious caution: be as critical in evaluating popular medical knowledge as in evaluating your doctor.

A marriage in which either partner abandons his own feelings and attitudes in favor of the other's isn't going to be an enduring marriage. A relationship between a doctor and patient in which the same thing happens won't be fruitful either. Each of the participants in this friendship should be changed by their encounter. To encounter each other and be unchanged by it is to have participated in a dead encounter.

You should leave the doctor's office feeling that all of your questions have been answered, and that you have met someone you would like to know as a friend if he weren't your doctor. Is he really approachable? Gods are not so approachable.

Some people say, "It's not important that my doctor be my friend. All I want him to do is treat me." All I can say is, if the doctor doesn't have the genuine concern for you that a real friend has, he will not get the information from you that will enable him to treat you effectively.

PATIENT'S CHECKLIST

First Phone Call
Does medical assistant give her name when answering phone?
Is she warm, concerned?
Do you feel rushed?
Are your questions answered?
Does she ask what's wrong with you, and if it's urgent?
Does she put you through to the doctor if asked?
Does she give you traveling instructions?
Does she answer your questions about the doctor's fee schedule, hospital affiliation, availability?

First Visit
Is office cheerful, comfortable?
Are you greeted pleasantly?

Does medical assistant inquire about your condition?

Does she inform you of the approximate delay, if there's to be one?

Is your chart made out promptly in an area of confidentiality?

Are the desks of medical assistants neat?

Are the medical assistants friendly, reassuring?

Are there appropriate reading materials, including magazines of general interest as well as health magazines?

Is there a "no smoking" sign, indicating overall concern for patients' health?

Is the waiting room crowded?

First Encounter With Doctor

Does the doctor welcome you or does he ignore your entrance, continuing to peruse his work or talk on the phone?

Does his consultation room meet the same criteria as the waiting room?

Is the doctor's desk neat?

Are you given close attention, or does the doctor interrupt to take calls, respond to his assistants?

Are you oriented by the doctor about the nature of the examination?

Do you feel rushed when talking to him?

Does he take a thorough history?

Does he show an interest in you outside of your presenting symptom?

Is he a good listener?

Does he seem to empathize with you?

Does he share his own background and interests?

Does he use jargon?

Does he smoke?

Is he obese?

Does he answer your questions freely regarding his medical training, hospital affiliation, emergency protocol, fee schedule?

Examination Room

Is the purpose of tests explained by medical assistant?

Are the tests done with apparent skill and concern?

Is the equipment modern or shopworn?

Does the medical assistant welcome and answer your questions?

Is the examination room clean, neat, modern?

Are delays in the examination room explained, or are you lost and forgotten?

Are there magazines in the pre-examination rooms?

The Examination

Does it proceed without interruption?

Does doctor offer information about procedures?

Does he answer questions to your satisfaction?

Does he proceed systematically and thoroughly?

Does he accept suggestions?

The Evaluation

Does doctor summarize his findings, note the data gathered, and explain his conclusions?

Does he put you at ease, or do you feel rushed?

Does he preach, talk down, give orders, speak quickly?

Does he encourage questions?

Does he use jargon?

Does he encourage you to call him in a few days, or whenever you feel the need?

Does he consistently and intensively follow up the data gathered?

3

Games Not to Play

■■

YOUR REACTION to illness is a big factor in your treatment and eventual recovery. Yet there has never been any kind of training in how to be an intelligent and self-helping patient. Consciously or unconsciously, we have learned how to behave as patients in the same way we learn how to behave in sexual or familial relationships. We're supposed to assimilate behavior by mystical intuition, when the truth is that in both sexual relationships and parental roles we would profit from less mystique and more consciousness-raising guidance. The same is true of our role as patients.

Our behavior as patients is rarely as helpful as it needs to be. Some of it is tolerable. Much of it impedes the healing process. Occasionally it can be downright dangerous.

A number of distinctive patient "types" have emerged from my feedback discussions during the last several years. Each "type" plays a role. Each role represents a coming to terms with the medical mystique and derives from a feeling of dependency, a need to adjust in some way to the problem represented by the authoritarian fatherlike doctor figure. Each of these roles is immature, antitherapeutic, and harmful.

WHAT KIND OF PATIENT ARE YOU?

Macho	denies illness
Closed Mouth	tests the doctor
Live-It-Up	it can't happen to me
Can't Be Bothered	next week, next month, next year
I-Need-Your-Love	my life is in your hands
Anything You Say, Doc	afraid to decide for yourself
I'm Done For	life is an illness
In and Out	time is better than health
You Made Me Sick, Doc	lots of my friends smoke, and *they* don't get heart trouble
Don't Hurt Me	God will cure me
You Can't Help Me	she's right; I can't if she won't let me
Cocktail Party	who needs appointments?
Tease	wait until I know you better

Make It Convenient	he's running scared
Don't Criticize Me	diverts attention from what's really bugging him
Do Something	don't just stand there; give me a shot
I Treat Myself	with all the wrong left-over medicines
Whip Me	father-doctor knows best
Don't Tell Me	ignorance is bliss

The Macho Patient: Denies illness, feels it's an evidence of weakness, can't relate to physicians, stays away from them unless symptoms are really disabling. The husband of a patient of mine was an executive who kept getting episodic heart palpitations, not often enough to convince him to see a doctor, just enough to scare his wife out of her wits. One day she called me to say her husband couldn't breathe. I told her to get him to the hospital. He had a rapid irregular heart rhythm that was difficult to control, although we finally succeeded. The problem could have been put under control much earlier with preventive medication such as digitalis. When I asked him why he hadn't come to me, the patient replied, "Doctors are for people who are old and sick."

Most macho patients are men, but women frequently exhibit the same behavior.

The Closed-Mouth Patient: Will withhold information, sometimes deliberately, to test the doctor's competence, and sometimes unconsciously, because of fear, shame, a desire to protect personal privacy, a need to deny illness, or a feeling the information isn't important. A woman came to me with indications of kidney failure, including swollen ankles and eyes. Lab tests supported the diagnosis. Appropriate treatment was instituted but she didn't seem to respond. I queried her exhaustively about her diet, medications, and history of infections. She vehemently denied taking any drugs. She didn't give me a clue. Finally, her husband told me that he had seen her at the medicine cabinet, taking a drug called phenacetin. He didn't think it had anything to do with the problem because he'd seen her take the pills sporadically. It had everything to do with the problem. In large doses, and over a long period of time, phenacetin can cause kidney failure. She had taken the medication because it had helped relieve her headaches. She continued to take it, despite my warnings to stop, on the grounds that it had never caused her pain. She died within the year.

The Live-It-Up Patient: Has no respect for his body, scoffs at health habits, pleasure is paramount—just wants to feel good. I had a patient who was jolly, portly, prematurely gray, a hyperkinetic businessman. He'd drink, in his words, "not too often, one or two before lunch, one or two before dinner, one or two after dinner." He smoked one to two packs of cigarettes a day, depending on how he felt. If he was tense, he'd smoke a little more, if not tense, a little less. He was sure he was doing nothing harmful because all his friends did as he did and it never bothered them. When his physical examination revealed minor changes on his cardiogram and a mild elevation of cholesterol, I told him, "George, you're really risking a coronary. All the risk factors are there." George scoffed at my warning. He died of a sudden heart attack while on a business trip to Paris.

The I-Can't-Be-Bothered Patient: "Too busy. Better things to do. Besides, it doesn't bother me that much." These were the reasons given by a young businessman who didn't want to attend properly to his gallstones. His health was basically good and the stones were causing only occasional gastric disturbances, so the surgery I recommended would have been optimal at that point. "I just don't have the time," he said. He came back several months later. His eyes were jaundiced. His urine had changed color. The pain in his abdomen was more frequent and severe. When the operation was performed, it was found that his gallstones had moved into the main bile duct, obstructing the flow of bile from the liver and thereby causing jaundice. His pancreas was inflamed. All these factors made the operation a stormy one. His recovery was complicated.

The I-Need-Your-Love Patient: In awe of the doctor, must constantly be reassured that the doc-

tor loves her, conditioned to feel that doctors have
her fate in their hands—if, God forbid, she should
in any way offend them. . . . An actress whom I
hadn't seen in three years came to me one day.
"What took you so long to come back?" I asked
her. "Why didn't you come for your checkup?"
She'd never missed her regular checkup in years
past. On her last visit it developed I'd recommended
that she have a skin mole removed. She'd gone to
the specialist I'd chosen but hadn't liked him because he didn't show her enough love. Another specialist removed the mole. "I thought you'd kill me
for not going to the man you recommended," she
said. She actually was afraid to tell me out of fear
she'd lose my affection.

The Anything-You-Say-Doctor Patient: Mostly
women, but my example in this case is a man. He
was an editor who had stayed with the same doctor
for years, even though the doctor failed to cure his
pain. "It's your arthritis," the doctor would tell him,
and treat him with vitamin B-12 shots. When the
pain became so intense that his family life was suffering, his wife brought him to me. The pain
sounded pleuritic in nature; it got worse when the
patient coughed or took a deep breath. X-rays of the
chest revealed a mass in one lung. It was removed
by surgery and found to be malignant. Fortunately
the cancer was limited to one lobe; several years
later there was no evidence of spread. What was so
frustrating was that the patient had abdicated his

right to question and doubt. Even though his family doctor had missed the diagnosis, it was, "Anything you say, doctor."

The I'm-Done-For Patient: Life is an illness, has a morbid involvement with his body and with death; whatever the symptoms are, they are the ritualistic announcement of the end. I had one patient who was, in all other respects, a perfectly lovely woman, gentle, sweet and bright. Her symptom was dizziness, which she brought to me at the beginning of my practice more than eighteen years ago. I examined her carefully and did everything required but could never locate any problem. Nor could the neurologist and ear specialist I sent her to. Today she still feels dizzy, she still says she's done for, as she has for the last eighteen years. She still seems to need the attention she gets from announcement of her imminent demise.

And I am still responding to her cry of "wolf."

The In-And-Out Patient: Time is more important than a thorough examination. A visit by her upsets the entire office. She storms in, advances on the receptionist, demands immediate service. "Get me in, get me out." What she doesn't know is that the office staff has scheduled appointments so that she can be obliged. If she has a cold, it's difficult for me to convince her that she should take off her blouse so I can listen to her lungs. "Just listen to me through the blouse," she says. Once, for lack of energy, she wanted "a pill or a shot or anything that's fast." I refused, of course, and told her that if she continued to carry on this way I'd have to stop trying to treat her. Which at least persuaded her to undress so I could examine her thoroughly. A rectal examination disclosed a carcinoma, which was causing her fatigue secondary to anemia and was later surgically removed. There is no evidence of spread of the malignancy as of now, but the prognosis remains guarded.

The You-Made-Me-Sick Patient: This man was a heavy smoker. His lungs were damaged. He required many diagnostic surveys. Once when he was in the hospital to receive inhalation therapy for his chronic pulmonary condition, he became very upset with me. "Look what's happened to me," he said, his tone implying I'd somehow made him sick. He knew lots of heavy smokers, he said, and none of them was in trouble. Shortly after his discharge from the hospital, he left me for another doctor. Not long thereafter a member of his family told me he'd developed an ulcer. He blames his new doctor for that. And he continues to smoke.

The Don't-Hurt-Me Patient: Some medical procedures cause discomfort. Good technique, and anesthesia when necessary, helps to minimize the pain. Nevertheless some patients will tolerate no procedure that involves any pain at all, and the likely result is that they'll eventually wind up with more pain than they were trying to avoid. A woman came to me complaining of discomfort in her lower leg.

It appeared to be an occlusion of an artery. I suggested she consult a vascular surgeon. She was shocked. In the past, every time I'd suggested different chemistries, such as a blood test, she'd resisted. But now the pain persisted to a point where she did go to the surgeon. He explained how he would apply a local anesthesia over the skin, make a small incision, insert a catheter, and then inject a dye into her arteries, all this to help him locate the obstruction. She was certain that the procedure would be painful. She refused. One day several weeks later I received a distress call from the patient. Her leg had changed color. The skin was mottled. The entire extremity felt numb. We rushed her to the hospital, where a bypass graft was performed. She had waited so long and had so compromised the tissue that the operation was touch and go. In addition to the physical pain that could have been avoided, she suffered the additional discomfort of being needlessly frightened.

The You-Can't-Help-Me Patient: A middle-aged woman complained to me that certain foods always gave her indigestion. She was allergic, she said, to a second set of foods. A third group gave her gas. As I reviewed her diet with her, and proposed various solutions, it became evident that she'd eliminated everything but water. She'd made up her mind she couldn't be helped; and that being the case, there was no way I could help her—although I tried.

The Cocktail-Party Patient: She gets her information from friends at gatherings—friends who are generous with advice. One of my patients began to wheeze a few years ago for no apparent reason. She'd never done it before, never had asthma or other respiratory ailments. Friends offered her antibiotics. She took them, continued to wheeze. Other friends suggested certain antihistamines. She tried these—no success. Finally she checked in with me. During routine questioning I asked her if she used oral contraceptives. She did. She'd started a few months before—at the time she started wheezing. We took her off the oral contraceptives; she doesn't wheeze any more.

The Teasing Patient: Each time an examination is performed she stops the doctor at a certain point. Each point reached is just a *little* further along toward the point the doctor must reach if he's to treat her responsibly. A woman came to me with a complaint of lower abdominal distress. I suspected some kind of inflammatory pelvic disease and suggested an internal examination. No, she said, not this time. The next day, she finally let me perform the examination, and consented only because she was running a high fever, which I convinced her was connected to her distress and probable infection. Sure enough, her ovaries and tubes were infected and inflamed. I put her on antibiotics at once, but the delay had been so long that she didn't respond to the treatment. Eventually she required a hysterectomy.

The Make-It-Convenient Patient: He was an independent businessman in his early seventies who did a lot of traveling. He had a vigorous sex life, which he had to protect at all costs. Periodically he would have trouble urinating. Examination disclosed a huge prostate, which was obstructing his bladder, causing him to retain urine. I recommended surgery. But it was never "convenient." He always had appointments in other cities, or deals he had to make. Actually, he was afraid of the surgery because of what he thought it might do to his sex life. I assured him it would do nothing, but he refused to believe me. His condition became so bad that in order to empty his bladder he required catheterization in each city he visited. Finally he was admitted to University Hospital in New York City; I told him he couldn't keep going the way he had been. He finally submitted to uneventful surgery—after which his keen relationships continued.

The Don't-Criticize-Me Patient: Diverts attention from what's really troubling him by attacking you for being too critical of him. One of my patients had cirrhosis of the liver from years of heavy drinking. If we talked about his drinking—or his smoking—he'd say, "Don't criticize me. You're attacking me. You're coming down hard on me." His remarks were a smoke screen to hide his shame. He was afraid of doctors.

The Do-Something-For-Me Patient: Needs some

tangible expression of attention; the medical "rites" must be observed. A woman came to me complaining of fatigue. She asked for injections of vitamin B-12. I suggested that we should talk first to see if we could find out why she was tired and then proceed with tests. She didn't have time for that and went to another doctor who would give her what she wanted. Several years later I found out that the woman had had anemia, that her doctor had continued to treat her with shots for her anemia, and that a stomach tumor had gone undiagnosed and had eventually killed her.

The I-Can-Treat-Myself Patient: His and her numbers are legion. They remember the same symptoms from a previous illness, wonder where that little bottle of pills is that the doctor prescribed then, find a bottle that seems to be the one—and wind up complicating their case. One of my patients, suffering from a strep throat, decided to treat herself with a left-over antibiotic. Not only was it the wrong medicine, not only did her infection fail to respond, but she developed a reaction to the antibiotic and wound up in the hospital.

The Whip-Me Patient: Passive, looks for a paternalistic situation in which father-doctor knows best. The more authoritarian the doctor, the more the doctor must really know, and the more, therefore, the doctor should be trusted. Of all the perversions of the doctor-patient relationship, this one troubles me the most. The patient seeks out the kind of doctor who will tell him with absolute assurance that these are the facts of his case, and that's all there is to it. To question the doctor is to demonstrate mistrust. That kind of certitude is a mask for ignorance. I was visited by a man who'd been having trouble urinating. His family physician had told him that the problem was related to his age. In other words, when you get older, that's the way it is, and you just have to be strong and not complain. I knew the physician as a cold, arrogant, almost sadistic man. In this case he was dispensing nonsense. The patient had a small carcinoma of the prostate. When I asked him why he had endured his treatment for so long, he said, "The doctor seemed to be so sure. I thought he knew exactly what I should do." The patient believed that because he wanted to; his doctor's gruffness and frequent failure to return calls only further convinced the man that he shouldn't question the expert.

The Don't-Tell-Me Patient: He won't listen to what a doctor tells him, and if he hears, he won't believe. He can't accept reality. A man in his early fifties, a carpenter by trade, developed a tiny black area on his toe, no bigger than a wart. For several months he did nothing but pick at the growth. He was a man who'd almost never been ill and had treated himself when he had been. The black spot got larger and began to ulcerate. Finally he saw a physician who diagnosed a malignant melanoma, a tumor that spreads quickly and widely through the body. By the time his leg could be amputated the malignancy had spread to his abdomen. A few months later he developed seizures, indicating that the tumor had spread to his brain. Throughout his illness the patient refused to discuss it. . . . "I don't want to hear about it. . . ." When finally confronted with the fact that he required cobalt therapy, he said, "That isn't so, it can't be so." He died believing that the radiation treatments had been to control his seizures. Technically he was correct, and there was a certain solace in knowing that he had spared himself the agony of realizing he had an illness that had no cure. But if he'd accepted reality at the outset and had that small black spot removed, he'd be alive today.

HOW DOCTORS SUPPORT PATIENT ROLE-PLAYING

What's common to all of these stories may be the life-jeopardizing ignorance and behavior of patients, but once again the mystique is the real villain—the mysticism with which medical knowledge is shrouded diverts patients from learning about their own bodies. We're all afraid of what we don't know. The examples I've given are extreme ones. But all of us are infected to a degree with the same fears that provoked such episodes.

Fear of the unknown is at the heart of the problem. To deal with it doctors often assume the posture of fathers, believing that the paternal role is comforting and therefore therapeutic. It does comfort, but sometimes at great cost. It confirms the patients' games—and the games "confirm" the mystique. Doctors assume patients want to be dependent because they see them in their dependent roles. It rarely occurs to either of us that we "validate" one another's roles.

If doctors were to stop and examine the evidence, they'd see at once that patients want to learn and are able to learn. The fact that patients don't ask questions makes some doctors believe they don't want to be given information, and they use this belief to justify not informing their patients. Or, as a variant of this justification, it's said that when patients ask questions about their condition they want reassurance, not factual information. I believe such assumptions by doctors have relatively little basis in fact—patients *do* want to be given information, and *do* want to be told the truth.

Doctors Thomas S. Szasz and Marc H. Hollender divide patient response into three categories: passivity, cooperation, and mutual participation. The idea of mutual participation is essentially foreign to medicine, they find. It's the active-passive relationship that's most common.

How can you move from passivity through co-operation to mutual participation?

All behavior is learned. Health behavior is learned. Behavior can be changed, including health behavior.

4

How to Be a Smart Patient

SEVERAL YEARS ago, the father of one of my patients was in a Memphis hospital, ill with cancer. He and his daughter—my patient—were extremely close. She'd visit him constantly, and on one of her visits she noticed he seemed more lethargic than his disease warranted. When she tried to relate her impressions to the consultants who were treating her father, she wasn't able to communicate with them. She determined to do something about that. From her father's nurses she learned what medication he was receiving. Then she looked up the medicines in the *Physicians' Desk Reference*, or *PDR*, which lists the different side effects of medication. She went back to the consultants and indicated, with knowledge, that certain of the drugs might be making him drowsy. This time, the physicians were impressed enough to listen to her. They subsequently changed her father's medication. In the last weeks of his life, her father was less lethargic and sleepy, and much more able to relate to those around him.

The woman who told this story at one of my feedback sessions was bitter about the experience. She described the doctors as "arrogant" and "haughty." Her parents had chosen the most important— that is, the "biggest"—doctors they could find. And throughout the treatment, the specialists had ignored the woman's mother, who was patently afraid of them.

To me, this story not only exhibits the medical mystique at its worst but demonstrates how the mystique can be successfully overcome. The magic word is "knowledge."

The knowing patient gets more respect. Doctors and their gatekeepers pay greater attention to him. His treatment, as a consequence, is more thoughtfully considered, and generally more successful.

It's in the interest of anyone who cares about his well-being to be a knowing *and* assertive patient. This chapter will try to show you how to become one. It will give you guidelines for assessing your own illness and help you deal with your doctor and his gatekeepers.

THE SMART PATIENT

Asks questions

Takes notes

Seeks additional information about his body, symptoms, disease

Says what's on his mind

Offers feedback: upsets, feelings, events, ideas, suggestions

Respects his body by health maintenance and restraint

Tries to be an observant, accurate reporter

Shares his experiences with other patients

Doesn't get impatient; recognizes that change takes time

Doesn't abdicate responsibility

Welcomes criticism

Leaves his physician for another one when relationship is antitherapeutic

Knows his rights as a patient

Knows his responsibilities as a patient

Trusts his feelings, and his ability to make judgments

To be a smart patient, you have to learn how to understand disease, how to recognize its symptoms, and how to understand your own reaction to illness. Health behavior is not something that's turned on when you get sick; it's operating every minute of your life.

If you're like most patients, you don't really know what a symptom is or how to handle it. You understand little about the natural history of diseases. Nonetheless, you are constantly making self-diagnoses and prescribing your own cures. You "confirm" these diagnoses and treatments by consulting with members of your family, friends, and co-workers. This tradition has its origins in folk medicine, and I'm not against it. But I say, let's do it competently and be aware of its limitations. Let's raise the level of folk medicine. Let's improve the understanding people have about illness.

Illness has different meanings for different people. Some of these meanings have little to do with reality. If that's the case, you're in dangerous waters. I once had a patient who was his mother's sole support. He was a meticulous man with an established routine. One day he failed to show for an appointment and hadn't been at his office all day. His colleagues were so worried they asked me to go to his home. I did. The door to his apartment was locked. I broke in with the superintendent of his building. There was my patient, stretched out on his bed. Beside him was a key, and a note that said, "This is the key to my bank vault. I coughed up blood." He had taken an overdose of sedatives. I called for an ambulance. We sped to a hospital. He almost died, but an artificial kidney machine saved his life. When he'd recovered sufficiently, I asked him to explain his behavior. He told me he assumed that the blood he had coughed up related to a previous illness, a bronchiectasis, and that he would likely require an operation; and that in turn would mean a prolonged disability, during which he'd be a burden to his mother. My subsequent diagnosis established that he didn't have bronchiectasis but a much less serious flare of bronchitis. He hadn't known or considered that there are many reasons why he might have coughed up blood. He's still with me as a patient five years later, a remarkably strong, independent human being who almost killed himself because he didn't understand what was happening to him, and made a self-diagnosis out of fear.

THE SIGNS BEFORE THE SYMPTOMS

People rarely think of illness as something you can prevent. Rather it's something that reveals itself by a symptom. As a result we diagnose disease almost always during its overt manifestations. But cancers exist in our bodies long before they reveal themselves. Heart disease, diabetes, and almost all other diseases incubate in similar fashion.

Can we find these diseases before they reveal themselves? The answer is most often yes. But it's usually contingent on an alert patient.

Basically, diseases can be predicted in certain individuals. More and more work is being done by researchers to identify "populations at risk." Such studies, for example, can help us flag persons with a high risk of developing coronary disease. You may feel perfectly marvelous, but if you have a high cholesterol or triglyceride count, or high blood sugar, or if you have hypertension, or smoke, or are overweight, you are part of the coronary-risk population. That doesn't mean you're definitely going to develop coronary problems, but it does mean that you're more likely to do so than the rest of the population. If you want to lead a long, healthy life you can then begin to take certain precautions.

Disease doesn't have to await presentation of the symptoms. A smart patient will help his doctor discover what diseases he should look out for. A history of cancer, heart disease, or diabetes in one's family should put a patient with any self-regard on alert.

You should be able to disclose to the doctor everything about your background, your family, its illnesses and your own, the nature of your work, nutrition, health habits, and sex life. You're saying to your doctor that you trust him. You're saying that you want him to become intimately involved in those aspects of your life he needs to know about in order to be able to discover the signs of disease before it reveals itself in symptoms.

Even when a piece of information seems only marginal to your health, you should give your doctor and yourself the benefit of the doubt and let him know about it. A journalist recuperating at home following an acute case of pneumonia told me by phone that her daughter was coming for a visit that day and would be bringing her two Siamese cats. Now normally one doesn't ask every patient, "Are you going to be visited by a daughter who'll be bringing two Siamese cats?" In this case, the patient had the awareness, and the confidence in me, to mention the fact on the outside chance that it might be important. It was important. If you're a lung patient and allergic to cats, they can trigger a dangerous bronchospasm—fit of coughing.

The signs your doctor is looking for are the everyday ones that, unless he is aware of them, will slip by unnoticed until they manifest themselves as problems. Consider cholesterol. It doesn't hurt. It doesn't make you feel bad. But it could be endangering your life. If during your examination you tell the doctor you eat a lot of red meat, butter, eggs, bacon, fried foods, use olive oil in your salad dressing, and drink quantities of milk, the doctor can explain why this diet can cause you problems. He will tell you how such foods leave residues of fat on the lining of the arteries and thereby impede the normal flow of blood.

READING YOUR OWN ILLNESS

There is no reason why you can't be aware of and learn to look at a symptom the way a doctor does.

I'm not suggesting you make a diagnosis of illness on the basis of a symptom. But you can put a symptom into context. Your doctor is supposed to use a logical, systematic approach to find out why your normal functioning has been interrupted. You can do this kind of analysis on your own before consulting with your doctor. Obviously, you're not going to treat yourself, nor are you going to pinpoint and diagnose your disease. But you will be providing invaluable service to yourself and your physician by helping to locate the area of illness.

Your doctor's strategy of treatment works as follows: He tries to define risks before signs, to note signs present before symptoms, to discover symptoms before disease and to get to or treat disease before disability.

A doctor's diagnosis of your illness is based approximately seventy to seventy-five percent on your history; fifteen to twenty percent on physical signs obtained during examination; five to ten percent on laboratory findings; and five percent on the clinical developments. Given these percentages, consider how important it is for you to communicate knowledgeably what it is that ails you, and for the doctor to encourage you in every way to do so and to listen carefully to what you tell him.

Suppose a young woman feels a sharp pain in the upper-right chest, and the pain increases with respiration, a deep breath, or a cough. This is a pleuriticlike pain. If she's using oral contraceptives, this pain could be caused by a pulmonary embolus secondary to thrombophlebitis. In simple language, a clot in the lung.

Suppose the woman doesn't tell the physician that she's using oral contraceptives. The doctor will be missing a vital clue.

Suppose the doctor hasn't told her of the possible side effects of oral contraceptives. The patient won't be alert to those possibilities.

The doctor *should* inform the patient. And the patient has the responsibility to ask the doctor for information, if it's not volunteered.

Your doctors can make a colleague of you by showing data on which a diagnosis is based and telling you their meaning. There's no reason, for example, why your doctor can't show you your cardiogram, and explain its patterns to you. I had one patient with a heart condition who was despondent because he felt he'd lost control of his life. When I showed him his cardiogram his interest immediately perked up. He could see by the upright T-wave on his newest cardiogram, as against an inverted T-wave on his earlier cardiogram, that his condition had improved. He was much more motivated to continue to take care of himself. To care *about* himself.

There are eight aspects to symptom analysis. None is mysterious. You're at least as capable of understanding them as a beginning medical student.

SYMPTOM ANALYSIS

1. Quality
2. Intensity
3. Duration (be as specific as possible)
4. Location (exact)
5. Radiation (how far the sensation spreads)
6. Influence on symptoms
   —What precipitates them: When? How?
   —What makes them worse?
   —What relieves the symptoms?
7. Association with other symptoms
8. Recurrence (history, how frequent)

Let's consider the headache. Normally what impresses you is the degree of your discomfort, and its duration. Both are important. But there are other things to think about: Is it a new kind of headache, different in the quality of pain, location, and duration than you've ever had before? If it's a lingering headache, is this the first one of its kind? Is the headache associated with any other symptoms? Does the headache mean anything in terms of your own or your family's background? A headache experienced by someone who has rarely been ill means something different from a headache experienced by someone whose family has a history of hypertension.

If you can write down these characteristics while you're experiencing the symptom, you'll be able to provide your doctor with a much more accurate report than if you rely on your memory.

In learning to view symptoms as a doctor does, you will come to understand the real criteria of his concern when evaluating what's wrong with *you* —and you'll be working together on it. Every symptom should be respected, but its meaning will be different depending on its history. There is nothing mystical or arcane about such knowledge; it belongs to you as much as to the doctor. Take the case of a patient who went to the mountains on a vacation and immediately experienced a bowel problem. He almost constantly felt an urge to defecate, but each time he tried he would pass little but water. Upon rising, he would feel the urge again. You might immediately think that the problem was a change in diet, water, schedule, or location—and all of these might be factors. But you should be thinking, as well, about the historical context of the problem. Was it the first time it ever happened? If so, it could be a serious problem—the first indication of an obstruction caused by a tumor. However, if the same thing has happened every time he's gone to the mountains, there's clearly less reason for concern. Similarly, if he's experienced the same problem in other circumstances, the symptom should be less worrisome. In this case, the patient was a television personality who was under a lot of tension. Tension by itself can change the bowel pattern in exactly the manner he'd experienced.

Age is another consideration in deciding how concerned to be in such a situation. The possibility of a growth is less likely in the twenties than in the fifties. By a certain age, it's unwise to dismiss difficulties with bowel movements as just another flareup of constipation. Many chronically constipated older people develop cancers on top of their problem, a situation that can be very deceptive. The important consideration here is whether there's something new about the problem. Is it, for example, even more difficult to have a bowel movement than it was before?

Years earlier, when he was a network correspondent, this patient had traveled widely in underdeveloped countries. The behavior of his bowel indicated there might be renewed presence of parasites and ova. Anyone who has ever had amoebas should have his stool analyzed from time to time.

All of these considerations should be kept in mind the next time you or a member of your family is chronically constipated. Is it an old flareup or a new experience? How old are you? What changes in your environment might be related to it? This list is by no means exhaustive, but it gives you a good start. And the same kinds of wide-ranging questions should be asked when you are aware of *any* symptom.

Certain symptoms require investigation the moment they appear. You wouldn't contact a doctor the first day you're constipated. But if you were to have blood in your stool, that's already meaningful regardless of persistence or duration or intensity. It might be significant, particularly if it's the first time it's appeared. Any sign of blood, whether it be in your urine or stool, or whether you cough it up, should be attended to at once. The same advice applies if you break out with numerous black-and-blue spots—a sign of internal bleeding.

A mild headache that lasts for an hour is, in all probability, insufficient cause for alarm. An excruciating headache, unlike any you've had before, that lasts for an hour should move you to get help. So should a mild headache that persists for a week.

Everything at this point depends on your educated perception of what's serious or dangerous, and your heightened awareness of the possible significance of what ails you. This doesn't mean that you'll respond to every symptom with the thought that it's serious or dangerous. To the contrary. As an informed patient, you'll have a more realistic outlook. On the other hand you won't be ashamed to assert yourself when you do call to describe your symptoms, because you'll know that you have the kind of information that a doctor needs to make the definitive decision about whether your condition is serious.

ALARMING SYMPTOMS THAT REQUIRE IMMEDIATE RESPONSE

Usually these symptoms are characterized by abrupt onset with severe intensity.

Neuromuscular
  Syncope:
    Fainting, coma, lethargy, confusion
    Vertigo, dizziness
    Headache, with stiff neck
  Eye symptoms:
    Can't see, flashes of light, severe eye pain, or sudden double vision
  Ear symptoms:
    Can't hear, severe, sudden ringing in ear, severe earache.
  Sudden weakness or paralysis in one extremity
  Seizure, convulsion
  Change in mental state or change in speech

Gastrointestinal
  Sudden inability to defecate
  Severe abdominal pain
  Blood in stool—indicated by black stool as well as more familiar bright-red blood in stool
  Inability to swallow
  Sudden, severe, profuse vomiting, with or without blood
  Profuse diarrhea

Genitourinary
Inability to urinate
Blood in urine
Profuse vaginal bleeding

Respiratory
Inability to breathe
Marked coughing, severe sudden cough out blood
Severe and profuse nosebleed
Marked discoloration of skin

Cardiovascular
Chest pain
Sudden rapid pulse rate
Irregular pulse, particularly very slow pulse

Skin
Sudden onset of black-and-blue marks in skin
Marked, profuse, and sudden sweating
Blue coloration of skin
Sudden very high or very low temperature

If you're a smart patient you'll also understand the effect of associations in the perception of symptoms. You may be responding to a headache you would otherwise ignore because a friend recently had a brain tumor. If a member of your family has recently suffered a heart attack, you'll tend to become much more aware of symptoms in the chest. The illness of a famous person produces an epidemic of self-concern; witness the enormous interest in checking for breast cancer after both Mrs. Ford and Mrs. Rockefeller had mastectomies.

Most important, a sophisticated patient will recognize his response to illness is much influenced by early models. If your mother was the kind of person who took you off to the doctor the moment you sneezed, hopefully you'll make appropriate allowances the next time you're tempted to worry about a sneeze. If, on the other hand, you were raised in a family that celebrated silent suffering, hopefully you'll discount such conditioned stoicism in deciding whether you should call your doctor.

Your style of behavior as a patient is determined by your childhood and family experiences, cultural background, educational level, socioeconomic status, and experiences in the medical world.

Researchers have established that while three out of four persons will experience symptoms of illness in a given month, only one will seek medical care. Jews who develop symptoms of illness tend to delay less in reporting them to a doctor than do Protestants, according to a report in *Social Science and Medicine,* and the reason given is the high emphasis on survival in the Jewish culture.

Different cultures respond differently to pain. A study in the *Journal of Social Issues* reports that Italians and Jews are "emotionally open" in their response to pain and likely to vocalize their upsets. By contrast, white Anglo-Saxon Protestant "old Americans" and Irish tended not to vocalize, or complain of, their discomfort.

A study of older married males in Providence, Rhode Island, reported in the *Journal of Health and Social Behavior,* noted variations in how people report illness. Italians reported minor changes in their condition while Anglo-Saxon Protestants complained only when they could no longer work or function with normal effectiveness.

This research doesn't necessarily mean that if you're Protestant you'll see a doctor less readily than if you're Jewish or Catholic. It means only that within certain cultural groups, certain statistical *tendencies* exist. You might as well be intelligently aware of them.

Just as your attitude to illness may vary depending on your economic conditions and cultural background, so may your attitude toward doctors. Again, this isn't to say that if you are Jewish, for example, you will necessarily reflect the attitude of Jews. But statistics tend to confirm a skeptical attitude toward doctors on the part of many Jews, who tend to go from doctor to doctor—a process which often fragments care, particularly if the primary physician is unaware of what's going on. Italians, on the other hand, generally tend to have a high degree of confidence in their doctor. Protestants, as a group, are highly motivated to cooperate with the doctor; their powerful work ethic keeps them from the doctor until they are very sick, and the same ethic supposedly drives them to get better as quickly as possible in order to return to work.

But all cultural tendencies tend eventually to be submerged in the encompassing American idiom.

The result is the "Americanized patient," who has characteristics of his own that we all share to some degree. He tries not to complain. He doesn't particularly want pity. He seeks approval. He tries to conform to what the physician expects of him. That's fine, providing the physician's expectations are that the patient should be an informed, interested partner in the health process.

The moment you begin, as such a partner, to reflect more thoroughly on your symptoms, you've added to your prospects for good health. At the same time, you should be aware that there's a certain psychological reaction to a more thorough involvement with your body. You may get somewhat upset at first. When I was a medical student, I experienced what we called "medical students' disease"—that is, I became something of a hypochondriac. More than once I thought I might have tumors. For a spell, I was sure I had Hodgkin's disease. When a dark spot, no bigger than a beauty mark, showed on my skin, I suspected it was malignant melanoma. Actually these false alarms were the normal accompaniment to learning about one's body and illness. Most medical students respond in similar fashion. There's no significant difference between their response and your own as you learn the nature of illness. There will be upsets and worries, most of them needless; when the experience is over, they will have been well worth the knowledge you've gained.

TREATMENT BY TELEPHONE

The telephone is a tool. Like any other tool, its value depends on its use. A knife can cut out a cancer. Or it can murder someone. The telephone can be a tremendous adjunct to care. It can also get you in trouble.

Diagnosis by phone requires some givens. The doctor must not only know what kinds of illnesses the patient on the phone has experienced but how the patient reacts to disease. The patient must be able knowledgeably and accurately to describe his symptoms. If those two elements are present the doctor can, on occasion, deal with a problem without having to ask his patient to the office or visit him at home.

Two added safeguards: if possible, a relative or friend should be on hand when the call is made, and should verify or amplify the patient's impressions for the doctor. The patient or his representative should also call back after treatment has begun, to report on the response.

The phone really must be used with the greatest caution. It's convenient for the patient to be "treated" this way. It should cost nothing. It's convenient for the doctor, as well, if he doesn't have time to see the patient. But the procedure is a partial one and can be dangerous, as dramatized by this story that surfaced during one of my feedback sessions. A patient had called his doctor to report a high temperature, a headache, and other symptoms suggesting grippe or influenza. The doctor told him that an epidemic was going around and that he should stay at home and rest. When the patient called back the next day to report he wasn't improved, the doctor prescribed an antibiotic. Three or four days passed. The headache became more severe. The patient became lethargic. He was rushed to the hospital, where a diagnosis of meningitis was made. His medication was changed to an appropriate antibiotic. The early symptoms of both diseases had been the same, but without a physical examination the doctor couldn't distinguish between them.

I rarely prescribe over the phone. Almost without exception I'll request the patient come in. The key factor, when I do prescribe over the phone, is what happens the next day or within the next two days at most. If the treatment I've prescribed hasn't changed the patient's condition, I absolutely insist that he come in.

But the patient himself may often know, without being told, whether he should see the doctor. The informed patient, the one who takes it upon himself to share more and more of the experiences and know-how of the doctor, and whose doctor helps him in this process, will begin to think as his doctor thinks in assessing illness.

Who should determine whether a problem can be handled by phone or requires an office visit?

Whenever you call and say you don't feel well, that's reason enough to be seen. If you have a symptom that has changed your functioning, you should be seen if you feel the need. Your responsibility here is to get across your need accurately and effectively to your doctor and his gatekeepers.

GETTING PAST THE GATEKEEPERS

Before you can get to your doctor, you must first deal with his "gatekeepers," the office personnel who assist him in his work. Once again, knowledge is the key—not only knowledge about your illness, but knowledge of the inner mechanics of your doctor's office: how it's run, how decisions are made, how your requests are handled and considered along with the dozens of others his office receives every day.

Whether you're calling your doctor or seeing him, "how long" has to be of prime concern for you.

Why is it that you can get through right away to some doctors, and have to wait hours before others return your call? Why do you wait interminably in some doctors' offices and hardly at all in others? What's to account for the differing natures of doctors' staffs? Are a doctor's gatekeepers a reflection of his personality? Does he know what's going on outside the gate to his inner office?

I am not talking here simply about matters of convenience; these things can affect the course of treatment. I have a friend who once called a specialist for an appointment. The specialist's secretary was so arrogant my friend couldn't tolerate her. He went to another specialist, who then mishandled the operation he performed on my friend. There's no guarantee that the first specialist would have done better, but he was a surgeon with an excellent reputation. Paradoxically, he also had a reputation for civility and probably wasn't aware of the effect his secretary had on his patients. But, undeniably, she was his responsibility.

And very often the doctor's gatekeepers *are* extensions of his personality. The gatekeeper receives guidelines from the doctor. With some doctors, the guideline amounts to "protect me"—presumably from the patients they're supposed to help. Fortunately, there are other doctors who will tell their gatekeepers that they're open to calls and interruptions. Unfortunately, many don't.

The medical mystique also pervades their gatekeepers at least as much as it does most of us. Many of these gatekeepers are filled with its myths and ideology and feelings. And they, in turn, disseminate the mystique. Gatekeepers are trained in the technology of office mechanics. They are generally not especially trained to focus on the patients' needs. Some of them develop such sensitivity and skill through experience. Others never do.

Even gatekeepers more comfortable with a passive patient will probably pay more attention to an assertive one. If a patient is actively assertive and knowledgeable he will receive attention more promptly than someone who is more docile.

Some patients will call the gatekeeper to ask for advice. Most gatekeepers are aware that they shouldn't give advice, if for no other reason than the legal implications, but some will respond anyway. Sometimes they'll copy the doctor's mannerisms. At one of my feedback sessions, a patient told how he'd called the office of an ophthalmologist to make an appointment for his son, whose eye had been injured in a collision. The doctor's gatekeeper offered him an appointment on a morning several weeks later. The father requested an afternoon appointment, explaining that his son didn't want to miss school. "Doctor *never* works afternoons," the gatekeeper responded in a sharp tone. My patient found another ophthalmologist.

What's important wasn't that the doctor was unavailable afternoons—maybe he did research or worked in a clinic. It was the manner and tone the gatekeeper used. Was there a welcome, open office there? Her tone of voice said there wasn't. She was disseminating the mystique of a deity, not a doctor or a doctor's representative.

Reversing the usual order, if you encounter a physician who's abrupt and curt, you'll likely see the same manner in his gatekeeper. True, sometimes the physician won't be aware of his gate-keeper's affecting certain mannerisms and would be upset if he knew. It's often a matter of poor communication between the physician and the gatekeeper. A doctor may say in an offhand way, "The schedule looks tight today." The gatekeeper will interpret that to mean the doctor doesn't want to be interrupted during the day, or can't see any more patients than those already scheduled. She becomes abrupt and rushed. Her interpretation is an overreaction—and bad for patient and doctor alike.

Patients do tend to assume that in every doctor's office perfect communication is the rule, that procedures are clearly set out, that everyone—and particularly the doctor—knows exactly what's happening. That's not always the case. The doctor should be aware of what's happening in his waiting room—how many patients are there, how long they've been waiting, which of them have urgent problems. But he must rely on his gatekeeper to report accurately to him and represent him. A doctor who's concerned above all with an efficiently run office may hire a gatekeeper who understands office mechanics but relates poorly to patients. A doctor whose primary concern is his patients' comfort will hire someone whose primary attribute is her ability to relate well to patients.

The gatekeeper, in effect, transmits the doctor's

values and beliefs. By their gatekeepers, in short, ye shall know them. . . .

We've said it before and we'll say it again: The patient who knows his body and is well-informed can be an effectively assertive patient; and this includes being so bold as to question the judgment of his caretakers, including gatekeepers who, like doctors, can make mistakes of judgment and timing. The gatekeeper may not open the gate for the patient who's always crying wolf. But a smart patient with a demonstrated knowledge about his situation will have rapport with the gatekeeper and if he says that a matter is serious, he'll likely be believed.

If you really believe your case requires a priority and find that the gatekeeper is unwilling to give it, you should ask her for a time when the doctor *is* available to speak to you. If the doctor still doesn't return your call and this happens more than a few times, your last resort is to tell the gatekeeper you'll have to find another doctor. You should indicate to her that if she doesn't act in your behalf, you will.

THE ANSWERING SERVICE

One way of reaching your physician when the gatekeeper is unresponsive is to phone after hours and contact the doctor's answering service.

Answering services may also reflect the doctor's mood and attitude. They, too, partake of the mystique—in which case they may tend to protect the doctor rather than help the patient.

The answering services used by doctors most often specialize in medical service. Their operators become knowledgeable over the years and learn how to glean enough information from a patient to know whether a situation is extreme and in any case to be able to report back to the doctor with accurate and meaningful information—which is their primary job.

Your responsibility with an answering service is the same as with an office gatekeeper: to impress the listener with the seriousness of your circumstance and your need to see the doctor, if that's the case. Being nasty or arrogant won't help. Being quietly, knowledgeably assertive will.

There's also no excuse at all for a telephone operator to be curt, arrogant, impatient, or unfriendly. Yet at the same time you should remember that you're talking to a telephone operator, not a medical person, and therefore not make unrealistic demands. You can, of course, ask and expect not to be rushed, not to be cut off, and to have your call attended to courteously and promptly. Nor are you obliged to put up with a service that in its interrogation and tone becomes so overzealous that it begins to mistake itself for the doctor. If such has been your experience, it's your right and obligation to report it to your doctor.

It would help considerably if, before calling the answering service, you were to write down on a piece of paper exactly what you want the doctor to know. Once you get on the phone, even with the answering service, your emotions begin to intrude. On that piece of paper you should try to detail the medical background that relates to your symptom, what exactly the symptom is, what you've done about it, why you're worried enough to be calling, and what you'd like from the doctor. Do you want to see him, or just talk to him, or do you want him to make that decision?

If you don't feel capable of making the call, have someone in your family, or some friend, call for you. The important thing is to make certain your message is given assertively—in a forthright, unapologetic manner.

If you haven't received a call back within a reasonable time—thirty minutes to an hour—you should call again. If you consider your case an emergency, say so, and indicate that you'd like a response from your physician within minutes.

Most of the good answering services know how to direct a patient when an emergency exists. On the assumption that your doctor may truly not be available because he's in transit, or operating, or away, you'd be wise to follow the procedure sug-

gested by the answering service, since it's one
established by your own physician. The answering
service, in this case, can call an ambulance and
direct you to the emergency room of your doctor's
hospital.

In any medical crisis, it's best to go directly to
the emergency room recommended by your doctor.
It is best to go for care rather than wait for care to
come to you.

IS WAITING REALLY NECESSARY?

Theoretically, there's no reason why anyone should
wait. If life went according to our plan for it,
there would be no wait at all. Unfortunately, of
course, it doesn't. There is, first of all, the matter
of common garden-variety human frailty. Your
doctor may get involved in personal matters or get
caught in traffic like anyone else. Unforeseen obligations are factors, too; on his morning hospital
rounds, the doctor might need to spend extra time
with a patient, or there's an emergency you can't
know about.

The important thing for you to measure is the
consistency of the pattern. If you have an occasional
wait in a doctor's office, that's a different and less
serious matter than if you wait every time. I remember one physician who actually said he felt
he was important enough for people to wait for

him. Consciously or unconsciously, he created the conditions that required his patients to wait. He'd schedule patients for 9:00 A.M. but did not arrive until 9:30 or 9:45. He felt it was good to have an office full of waiting people. It made *him* feel good—which isn't precisely the idea.

My own patients have been critical of me for long waits at the office, and have expressed their dissatisfaction at feedback sessions. I've tried to do something to solve the problem, and I've also explained to them the reasons for many of the delays. For example, I prefer to have patients wait in the office rather than wait several weeks for an appointment. Many doctors leave a gap in their schedules to be filled by emergencies or other unexpected occurrences. I do too. But there also are patients who have a sudden need to see the doctor, not so much because there's a physical emergency but because they need the reassurance of a visit. I find it unreasonable to tell this kind of patient that I can't see him for three to four weeks. If someone has a cough for several weeks, a few more weeks may not matter. But they also may. You can never be sure. Suppose it turned out to be a serious disease? The solution I've reached is to ask my patients to call half an hour before they're supposed to arrive for an appointment and to ask how my schedule is running. That system has gone a long way toward eliminating waiting time in my office.

Again, the key element is that you should assert

yourself in these matters. Speak up, be critical, ask questions. There's nothing infallible about a doctor or his staff, or sacrosanct about his office. If you find you're with a doctor who treats you as though you're in the lap of the gods, your role simply being to follow along, then I suspect you should say, "That is not the doctor I would like." Or if you like your doctor but find his staff cold and difficult to communicate with, you should say something to the effect of "Look, I think certain things could and should be done that you're not doing. And I'd like to make some suggestions." You should feel as free to make such suggestions as though you were part of the family. *A* part?—you're *the* part.

HOUSE CALLS

Treatment by telephone has become so commonplace in recent years that it's given rise to an almost mythic feeling about earlier times, when old-fashioned horse-and-buggy doctors knew all their patients and made innumerable house calls at any and all hours. The presumption is that these doctors gave health care far superior to present-day doctors. There's no real evidence to support this notion. Dr. John Kosa in *Social Science and Medicine* writes, "The old time general practitioner who went from apprenticeship or from a proprietary medical school into practice must have been rather wanting in skills, knowledge and confidence. His examination and treatment procedures were often outright negligent. His ethical deportment generally gave rise to more, not less, criticism. And his relationship with the patient must have been just as impersonal, or even anonymous, as the case is today. The myth nevertheless has strong hold over our imagination, because it properly expresses the deepseated and eternally human desire the public has for a charismatic leader, or for that matter, for the medical man who can heal with a pure, placebo effect of charisma."

You have the right to your doctor's presence at any and all times in an emergency. But your home isn't the appropriate place. The doctor's office is a better arena by far, and the emergency room of the nearest hospital is the best of all. There they have equipment to restart the heart, if necessary, to give intravenous treatment, to keep blood pressure normal, to administer oxygen or whatever medication is required. If any of these will eventually be required, then the doctor's visit to your home is at best a waste of time and at worst a dangerous delay.

A patient called me who had had a heart attack ten years before. He told me he'd fainted and felt weak. I told him to get to the hospital immediately. His wife took him in a taxicab. When he arrived, he went into cardiac arrest. He was shocked back to life. If I'd gone to his home, he would be dead.

Most doctors, I think, share this feeling about

house calls. And I think most doctors would agree with Dr. Carroll L. Witten, past president of the American Academy of Family Physicians, who has said, "It is rare to find a real emergency that can be handled adequately or with dispatch by a physician making a house call."

There are two types of patients who ought to be treated by house calls:

> 1. The truly bed-fast patient of any age; for example, those recuperating from a stroke, terminal patients or patients who must have total bed rest.
> 2. The patients with acute and infectious diseases that make them too ill to leave home.

Patients too often wait until nighttime to call their doctor. They've had symptoms throughout the day but haven't called. Night makes the symptoms seem more ominous. A smart patient telephones promptly as the symptom appears; he does not wait until midnight. He also keeps in mind that disease takes its own time to develop. The prodromal, or premonitory, symptoms can be *very* nonspecific. The smart patient will respond to the symptom even though there are no clear indications of exactly what's wrong. Not to do so is to risk your life.

A few years ago a man I'd met on a vacation came to New York for a wedding. As we'd become very friendly, I'd planned to see him socially. But when he called me it was to tell me he had a severe chest pain. I recommended he be taken right away to an emergency room. He refused and insisted that I come to his hotel. He didn't want to miss his cousin's wedding. I went to his hotel room with my electrocardiogram machine. Everything seemed fine: blood pressure, pulse, cardiogram. We reacted in opposite ways. He said he was in good enough shape to attend the wedding. I thought he should go to the hospital. He went to the wedding. At 3:30 the following morning he telephoned me to say he had a severe, crushing pain in his chest. I told him he was having a heart attack. I arranged for an ambulance. By the time I got to the hospital he was in the cardiac-care unit. He was lucky to have survived.

If a patient at home needs the emotional support that a doctor's presence there would give him, then the doctor should arrange for it. There are services available. Almost all medical societies have a staff of participating physicians to make house calls. One of them can make an examination, then communicate with the regular physician to decide what course of action to take.

The sensitive—as well as smart—patient knows that his doctor has a responsibility to him and all other patients to maintain a good frame of mind and physical condition. The doctor has a responsibility to preserve his resources. If he makes a call during the night that lasts several hours and doesn't get a good night's sleep, his work the next day has got to suffer.

The question of the house call—to make it or not to—is really a question for both doctor and patient. They've got to *talk,* to decide it jointly on realistic terms—not by the whim, or for the indulgence, of either.

THE SELF-HELPING PATIENT

There's a lot you can do to make your visit more efficient. By efficient, I don't mean using as little of the doctor's time as possible. I mean a visit in which you feel that all of your problems and needs have been carefully considered.

I'm a great believer in lists. Many doctors disparage patients who come to them with a written list of symptoms, or a digest of the family's medical history, or even an old family history given to another physician. They wonder if the patient isn't overly concerned with his health. I can understand this attitude, because such list-making isn't very common. But I hope that doctors would encourage their patients to make lists before their visits. It's good for both doctors and patients.

The patient who visits the doctor is under an emotional strain. He's nervous about what ails him. He wonders if it's serious, if the treatment will be painful, or costly, if he'll have to miss work or be hospitalized. Often, he feels badly. Add to these physical and psychological burdens the nervousness imposed by the tempo of the doctor's office and you have a person who probably won't communicate with full efficiency.

How many times have you heard yourself say to your doctor, "I forgot what I wanted to tell you"? And how many times, after your visit, have you remembered what you wanted to say? And surely you've experienced instances where your body seems to behave something like your automobile when you take it to the mechanic—the malfunction you want corrected strangely—and briefly—disappears. A full written description will help overcome those problems.

Many patients say they don't like to put things in writing. They think they may make a mistake or sound foolish. But often it's just because they've never been encouraged to do so. If the doctor would suggest the practice, and then welcome the result, the reluctance would quickly disappear.

What you write down—and what you eventually tell the doctor—should be as specific as you can possibly make it. Earlier, I suggested that you should attempt to note the characteristics of a symptom as it shows itself; that's the time when you should commit your observations to paper. If you tell your doctor that the heartburn you've experienced was more severe than any you'd ever had before, that's different from, "I've been having heartburn."

If necessary, you should come to the doctor's office with someone who can help relay symptoms and facts that you think you might forget. Such a precaution might be a good idea, in addition to a written list, if you're the kind of person who reacts adversely just to being in a doctor's office. For some people, emotion can obliterate memory. One woman came to me who couldn't remember the hospital where she'd recently had surgery or the surgeon who had performed it.

Again, you and your doctor work best in a partnership. You help yourself by joining it without reservation—confiding your stresses, worries, and secrets—providing, of course, that your doctor has made his equivalent commitment to the partnership.

If the partnership becomes a power struggle in which either of you tries to gain the upper hand, both of you are lost. If you ask your doctor not to be disease-oriented but to consider you as a whole person, you must do no less yourself. Hidden feelings are part of the mystical caricature of what a good patient should be—strong, controlled, and uncomplaining. Neither you nor your doctor wants you to fall apart, but it's important for him to see you as you are. If you are really worried about a symptom, the best way to convey that fear is to let it out.

If you become upset or angry with the doctor, you've got to tell him. The quickest way to impair your relationship with your doctor is to brood about a problem or let it fester. He won't know you're upset unless you show him or tell him. Only then can he make an adjustment.

Face it—you're as susceptible as the rest of us to illness from emotional causes. Boredom, loneliness, and anxiety can and do cause physical problems. Your health depends as much on how well you handle stress as it does on your ability to resist germs.

A smart patient is aware of his doctor's expectations, indeed, asks him what he expects. Like the doctor, he ought not to be afraid of his own humanity, of revealing the defects and weaknesses he's struggling to overcome. He sees the doctor as a person like himself, imperfect and mortal.

You and your doctor have probably been enacting roles that were first fashioned thousands of years ago and have been evolving and solidfying ever since; these set roles serve neither you nor your doctor. The only way for you to receive optimum care is to inform and assert yourself. The next step in ridding your relationship of the medical mystique is to learn how to talk to your doctor.

5

Patient Talk

IN JANUARY of 1974 *Glamour* magazine printed an editorial titled "Why Don't You Ask More Questions This Year?" It told the story of a young woman who visited her gynecologist for a pap test and breast examination before leaving for Europe on a six-month visit. What prompted her visit was a tiny lump she'd detected in her right breast. But the doctor assured her she was fine. The question then not unnaturally arose in the woman's mind, well, what do you do? Figure he's the expert and forget all about it, or do you tell him you thought you felt a lump and ask him to recheck the spot? The woman went off without questioning the doctor, but instead of staying away for six months, she remained away for a year. On her return she made an appointment to see her gynecologist, and they were both surprised and upset to discover a lump of considerable size in the same area where she'd thought she'd detected one earlier. A radical mastectomy was performed. It was generally agreed that had there been earlier detection, the extreme surgery could have been prevented.

Once again, we have a story that gets to the heart of the matter. A doctor enveloped in the medical mystique. A patient too timid to ask questions. Result: a medical error that could have been avoided. To look for human villains is to miss the point. It's the mystique that must be blamed.

The avenue to a more humanistic and thus more effective medicine is communication.

Saying communication is a two-way street is a cliché. Still, it's nowhere more applicable than in medicine. If a doctor who's attempting to communicate doesn't get his message across, his effectiveness will be impaired no matter how superb his craft. His patient won't understand the nature of the problem and the prescription for cure. If the patient doesn't communicate fully to the doctor, valuable clues are hidden that, at a minimum, could make diagnosis easier and speed the treatment progress. In extreme cases those clues mean the difference between life and death.

Doctors are unaware that they haven't communicated well. They assume that because they're speaking, the patient who is listening will automatically understand what ails him and responsibly follow instructions. It's a poor assumption. The patient may leave the doctor's office puzzled about his condition and without a commitment to pursue the recommended course of treatment.

How is it that two people with such an urgent need to communicate are often incapable of doing so?

Emotion can literally block understanding. One of my patients, a woman with severe heart disease, simply couldn't hear me when I explained why she had to go into the hospital. She was worried about what would happen to her children and her job. I only learned about the problem later when she brought it up at a feedback session.

Different needs and motives are as great a deterrent as emotion. If a doctor is interested solely in getting a patient in and out of his office as quickly as possible, but the patient is anxious about his health, the needs of these two people will be so different that there will be a communications turnoff. Or perhaps a patient's emotions are reflected through bodily symptoms, and he wants to talk about some disturbing relationships but his doctor has no interest—scorning the role of surrogate psychiatrist. Result: another turnoff.

When a doctor wants to control the relationship, or when he can't countenance criticism, his patients may be afraid to communicate with him for fear they might displease him. Some doctors feel that if they're questioned about procedures, their worth or skill as an expert is somehow being undermined —even though the question may be a simple request for information rather than an expression of doubt. In such circumstances, the doctor *does* manage to communicate his attitude toward questions, and silences the patient.

Another communication failure occurs when doctor and patient haven't worked together to make a decision. An order for a low-salt diet, for example, can seem like an arbitrary edict. The patient feels that a decision so basic to his everyday life is one he should have had a part in. He resents the doctor's authoritarian approach, and consequently doesn't maintain the diet.

I'm loud and clear about nonsmoking. My patients know that. I once told a patient with chronic lung disease not to smoke any more. She went home and told her son that I'd ordered her to cut it out simply because I was on a crusade, and not because it was necessary in her case. That was a mistake on my part. We had not, in the truest sense, come to the decision together. As a result she didn't see how a message I gave to everybody related particularly to her.

Communication problems can be compounded when the patient is a woman and the doctor is a man. When there's illness in the family, some doctors discuss it more easily with a father or husband than with a wife or mother. It shouldn't be a factor—but it often is. Some doctors also tend to be protective and paternal with women. Chivalry that blocks communication is out of place in a doctor's office. A woman, after all, has as much right as a man to know the truth about her condition; she's surely as capable of dealing with the truth as a man is.

Another indication of this male bias in medicine is the attitude toward the prospect of sterilization. Until recently, concern for the male ego made ligation of the woman's tubes a far more frequent procedure than a vasectomy on a man.

Women can, of course, complicate the communication problem by attitudes they bring to a doctor's office. One of my patients would never let me look at her breasts. She insisted I examine her underneath a sheet. Part of the examination of the breasts is observing the contours to establish whether there are any irregularities, indicating a growth. This woman was too frightened of her body to allow this. Today, thanks to the women's movement and increasing candor in the media, patients are becoming increasingly familiar and comfortable with their bodies. But to the extent that mystery remains, it's a marked and dangerous impediment.

Finally, some doctors just plain don't listen. They may hear what their patient is saying, but the message isn't getting through. They're preoccupied. They may be thinking about another patient.

A patient who's repetitious, who isn't direct about

what's bothering him, can, it's true, be a bore. But the doctor is obliged to pay special attention because of the requirements of his work.

Some doctors talk when they should be listening. Several times during my feedback sessions, patients have told me I interrupted too much. When one interrupts, it's a sign he's thinking ahead, he's not listening as acutely as he needs to.

He's also not giving another valuable medium for communication a fair chance. Most of us abhor silence. We feel it should be filled with conversation. But if there is no silence, there are no moments when people can reflect on what's just been said, and no integration of new knowledge.

MEDICAL JARGON

Even if doctor and patient were intellectually and culturally identical, there would still be an obstacle to good communication between them—language.

Language can be ambiguous. We all know that. But ambiguity can be much compounded in medical matters. When a doctor talks about a tumor, what does he mean? Is a tumor the same thing as a cancer? Could it become a cancer? A few years ago I found a polyp in the rectum of one of my patients; I told him he might have a "tumor." Several weeks passed; my patient, I discovered, had not reappeared for the examination I'd suggested. I called him. "Well, you said it was a tumor, so I'm not too worried," he told me. At that point I informed him that some tumors had malignant potentials. Once my language became more precise, my patient responded appropriately. Happily, the tumor was benign.

Suppose you're told to take one tablet four times a day. That leaves several unanswered questions: do you take the tablet before, or after, meals? Do you take it with, or separate from, other medication? Can you drink alcohol when you take this medication or must you avoid it completely? For how long do you continue the medication?

At a feedback session I heard of a man with epilepsy who was told to increase the dosage of his medication every Wednesday. His not unreasonable interpretation was that he should take an extra quantity that day and forgo the medicine on other days. The doctor failed to spell out that he meant increase the *weekly* dosage each Wednesday and continue through on each day of the week until the next Wednesday, etc. Not surprisingly, this case of shorthand jargon caused trouble.

When jargon, instead of simple English, appears on prescription labels, you have a problem. A recent study reported in the *Journal of the American Medical Association* demonstrated that *not once* were prescription labels interpreted uniformly by all patients. Of five prescriptions, the frequency of errors of interpretation ranged from nine percent to sixty-four percent.

I once told a patient not to eat salt because of a liver disease that caused her to retain fluid. Other spices were all right, I said. "Garlic?" the patient asked. "Fine," I replied, whereupon the patient started seasoning all her food with garlic salt.

Ambiguity and imprecision are common, perhaps inevitable—and therefore excusable. What can't be excused or tolerated is the use of medical jargon with patients. As one patient of another doctor put it, "Nobody should blame the doctor if he doesn't fix them up right away—or maybe never. But things would be better if we always knew what the hell he was driving at—and not in big words, either."

The vocabulary must be free of *technical* words that might confuse. A patient of mine didn't understand the word "palpitations." It was quickly clear when I asked if his heart had ever skipped a beat.

There are several ways to describe a disease, and one may be more meaningful than another. I had a woman patient who, so to speak, liked to live it up. She'd had a stroke, which we'd been able to pull her through, but she would not take my advice to slow down and take care of herself. I told her she'd had a thrombosis; I talked about the possibility of another one, to no effect. Even talking about a possible blood clot in the brain had no impact. But when I used the phrase "hardening of the arteries," the effect was profound. In her lexicon, *that* was serious. She immediately began to cooperate in her care. I'd said the same thing in three different ways, but only one of them had worked.

The 1973 report of the Commission on Medical Malpractice stated that a patient is entitled to know both the potential benefits and dangers involved in any treatment. Only with such knowledge can a patient fairly decide whether or not he wants the proposed treatment. He also has the right to know what the consequences might be if he refuses the proposed treatment. And he has the right to hear them in clear and untechnical language. "It is the physician's duty," the Commission said, "to translate technical terms into language the patient can understand so that complete communication can in fact be achieved."

Jargon, lingo, may often be used to impress a patient. It may impress him, but it surely confuses him. It's a different language than he's ever heard before. It reinforces the image of the expert whose thinking is inaccessible to the patient, and it mystifies meaning.

A doctor may say, "You have an atrial fibrillation and I hear a diastolic murmur with rumblings to the apex of your heart." Translation: "There's a change in the rhythm of your heart. There's a sound that's being caused by a narrowed valve between one chamber of your heart and the other."

Or, the doctor might say, "You have diffuse wheezes and rhonchi throughout your lungs, associated with diffuse areas of atelectasis." Translation: "You have some spasms of the breathing tubes, with some mucous accumulation, and this is plugging up your air sacs."

Or: "There is apparently a niche, a crater on the GI series, which is associated with hyperperistalsis and hypersecretion." Translation: "You've got an ulcer, and some increased acid in the stomach."

Or: "There is a calculus which is causing a hydroureter, and a hydronephrosis." Translation: "You have a stone in the kidney, which is causing the tube to balloon up above the blockage."

The patient receiving messages in jargon is understandably bewildered and often frightened. He fears what he doesn't know. Even when the doctor explains what he's talking about, matters may not be much better if the explanation is misleading. Suppose a doctor explains to a patient that an "atelectasis" means a collase of the lung behind a small mucous plug, but doesn't specify that only a small segment of the lung is involved. The patient visualizes the collapse of an entire lung—and the doctor wonders why he is frightened.

The passive patient who just sits there in silence compounds the problem. Rarely will such a patient inform a doctor that there's something he doesn't know. He's afraid to say, "I don't understand." Or else he imagines that he understands more than he does.

The communications problem in medicine today is not so much that people are without information. They have a great deal of information, thanks to the media, but they have either assimilated it poorly or taken it out of context. Their information isn't complete enough for a clear dialogue with their physicians. They have a medical vocabulary, but the words often don't mean the same thing to them that they mean to their doctors.

"Colitis" in lay terminology is quite different from colitis in medical terminology. For you, colitis may mean an irritable bowel, with alternating constipation and diarrhea, an indication of poor bowel habits. But to the doctor, colitis might refer to an inflammation of the bowel lining or any one of several other meanings.

"Congestion" usually is taken to mean a cold or some kind of bronchitis. To a doctor, congestion may describe a condition of heart failure in which fluid has seeped into the lung. The seriousness of the two conditions can scarcely be compared.

Naturally, you want to know what's wrong with you. Too often a doctor responds with a label. This may satisfy you—at last you know what to *call* your problem when asked about it. But you may not understand it—and that's bad. Even so common a word as "cholesterol" can mean almost nothing unless it is expressed in terms of elevated fat levels in the diet that can lead to hardening of the arteries.

I once listened to a house physician explain to a patient that he was to be given an IVP or intravenous pyelogram that would help us learn why he was experiencing severe pain in his loin, high up under the ribs. The procedure involved the insertion of a dye in a vein, which would travel through the kidneys and eventually be eliminated through the bladder.

"What do you think that means?" I asked the patient.

"That my tissue is going to be stained," the patient replied. He was understandably upset, until I told him that the clear liquid inserted in his veins would show up as white on an X-ray, would outline the structure of his kidneys, show how the urine passes from the kidneys to the bladder, and eventually leave the body—without a trace of having been there.

AN END TO MYSTICAL MEANINGS

Since it's the medical mystique that impairs communication, it follows that improved communication would do much to eliminate the negative aspects of the mystique. A free-flowing communication between doctor and patient implies a humanistic, caring physician and a confident, assertive patient. The problem is to get each of them from where they are to where they ought to be.

Somehow it must be conveyed to the doctor that you are capable of understanding a great deal about what ails you and what you must do to get well.

Somehow it must be conveyed to you that you are entitled to ask questions and get answers you understand. You must not, I repeat, treat the doctor like God.

Communication is freest when feelings of inequality have been neutralized. As long as doctor and patient operate according to the negative aspects of the medical mystique, in which the doctor-gods control their pastoral flocks, that isn't going to happen. At the same time, we don't want to set patients up as control figures in an adversary relationship with their doctors. If your doctor is someone you feel you have to control, you may be better off leaving him.

The only control either way that's needed in a medical relationship is the control by the patient of what happens to his body. He should feel that he can control the symptoms that are bothering him, not just by going to a doctor and doing blindly what the doctor tells him to, but by being an active participant in his treatment.

David Aspy, a humanistic psychologist, uses video tape to measure how people relate to one another, and his technique can be applied to physicians as well. One measurement is the quality of the doctor's voice as an indication of his interest in the patient. If the voice is flat and monotonous, his interest is apparently not very great. If the voice matches the patient's in tone and energy, it's an indication that he's empathizing with the patient. The content of the doctor's response can also be measured. If he enriches the meaning of the patient's experience with the addition of some appropriate comment, it's a sign he's communicating well. You don't need any electronic apparatus to fix your doctor's response. It's not so hard to tell whether he's paying attention or not, and whether he's really interested or merely tolerating the experience.

There are other simple measures of a doctor's willingness to communicate.

Does he view positively your ability to learn and be informed? If so, his instructions will be fat with explanations. He will presume nothing about your understanding.

Does he encourage questions, or does he give you the feeling that you're being cross-examined? His own questions shouldn't be delivered in rapid fire. You're not on the witness stand and he isn't the district attorney. You should be given a chance to express yourself fully, in your own manner, and at your own pace.

Has he created an environment and mood in his office that encourages your full participation?

Does he emphasize important concepts? Does

he pause to give you a chance to take it in and come back with questions?

All these go into determining how favorable the climate is for healthy communication. Now let's look at some specifics.

DIALOGUES WITH YOUR DOCTOR

Doctors, first of all, must be made aware when they're not communicating. If you don't understand what your doctor's telling you, tell him that you don't.

Medical knowledge can be simply expressed; it is not so complicated or sacred that it can't be shared.

When a doctor explains something to you, it's an excellent idea to repeat back at once what your understanding of that explanation is. Repeat the physician's instructions in your own words. Your physician would also do well to repeat, at least once, any instructions he's giving. He might also be wise to quiz you several weeks later to be sure your understanding has held.

Even if you and the doctor have repeated his instructions, it's possible that you'll soon forget what he told you. Two British researchers have established that patients are likely to forget as much as one-third of what's said to them. What the doctor's telling you is in competition with a lot of other things you're asked to remember. What he's telling you may also frighten you. If you don't forget entirely, you may only selectively remember. Don't worry that your doctor may be upset with you for forgetting. Call and ask him to repeat the instructions.

One way to avoid problems is to write down his instructions. I now make sure that a pad and pencil are always available when I talk to my patients. Some doctors rely on sets of printed instructions.

Always ask about your choices. This is particularly true in terms of surgery, but it's relevant in all cases. You must know your options. You should ask, "What's going to happen to me if I do nothing?"

Remember that you have a right to be upset. People tend to wonder, did I say something to antagonize the doctor? Is that why he's so abrupt with me? You can't let unspoken worries like that bottle you up. You don't have to become emotional to communicate well with your doctor, but you have to be able to say those things that sometimes only emotion will wring out of you. That's true of all of us.

Our society teaches us to be nice, gentle, and pleasant. We're educated not to make waves. We want things to be calm and peaceful. It's not a real calm it it's hiding something turbulent. People who are anxious to stay cool in their relationships generally will be especially concerned about staying calm with such an awesome presence as their doctor.

The medical mystique has served to exclude emotion as an aspect of communication. Patients are afraid to show emotion in the very place where they most need to show it. Your anger may not only be an invaluable clue to your illness, it can also be an aggravating factor. I once had a patient who believed he'd been given a raw deal in an area of his life and that I had been an agent of his illness. He let his feelings fester. One day they poured out. "I didn't make you sick," I told him. "People do get sick on their own. But your anger is making you worse."

Once he was willing to confront the source of his anger, he could also understand why *our* relationship was deteriorating. Once he acknowledged that anger was an acceptable emotion, the arthritis that had been aggravated as a consequence of his anger began to recede.

If you're angry with your doctor, or with his gatekeepers, or if you're upset with the progress of your care, you must let those feelings out. You must not think that you should be on your best behavior with your physician if your best behavior doesn't reflect what you're really feeling. Relationships only fester if upset and anger aren't expressed (which doesn't, of course, mean regressing to a childlike behavior of becoming neurotic). But if you're going to express emotion, let it out. Don't repress it or falsify your feeling. When your head and feelings work together, you can express emotion without being arrogant or self-centered or cruel to another person.

Here's a sample exchange:

DOCTOR: I want you to take this medication three times a day.

YOU: What will it do? I don't really feel I understand what's wrong with me—

DOCTOR: I told you. You have symptoms of heart failure.

YOU: But you haven't gone into the details for me.

DOCTOR: Do you really think you'd understand them? You're not a doctor, you know.

YOU: I think if you'd explain them in clear and simple language, I'd understand. Just try me . . .

Or suppose the doctor tells you to eliminate salt from your diet:

YOU: That's impossible. I don't have much money and I have very little time at lunch. I have to eat in a place near my office, and their food is already prepared. I can't ask them to cook especially for me.

DOCTOR: In that case I can prescribe a diuretic.

YOU: What's that?

DOCTOR: It's a medicinal substance that increases the volume of urine you excrete.

YOU: Which helps get rid of salt?

DOCTOR: Exactly.

YOU: Now you're talking.

Say what's on your mind. If you feel the doctor has rushed you, say so. If you feel confused, say so. If you feel your questions aren't being answered, say so. If you want to know more, say so. If you disagree with the therapeutic program, say so. If you can't follow the therapeutic program, for whatever reason, good or bad, say so. If you want a less directed approach, say so. If you want a stricter, firmer, more directed and disciplined approach, say so. Your life may depend on it.

Take time to reflect. If you can't sort out all of your feelings during an initial encounter, state them when they become available to you.

You can be assertive without disrupting your relationship with your doctor. The key is to be confident with your new knowledge. You now know how a doctor's office operates. You're aware of the dynamics between a doctor and his gatekeepers. You're informed about your body. You know how to ask questions. You can find out the different reactions to drugs by looking them up in the *Physicians' Desk Reference,* which can be obtained in most libraries. When you do have a disagreement with your doctor or his staff, you'll now be able to explain your viewpoint.

A patient of mine with a mass in her breast went into the hospital for a biopsy. When the nurse came by with the traditional consent form, the woman refused to sign it unless the form was amended to specify that the authorization was not for any and all procedures that her surgeon might consider necessary. The patient was knowledgeable, she knew the options, and she preferred to take the surgical process one step at a time despite the risk of additional anesthesia. She was not against a radical mastectomy if the mass was found to be malignant, but she wanted to know what the findings were before she would permit the surgeon to go ahead.

The only way you'll be heard is if you're knowledgeably firm about what you want. You have a tremendous obligation once you assume some responsibility for your own well-being, but once you're reasonably sure of your position, you should be quietly secure about it. One of my favorite feedback stories is about a patient who, for religious reasons, insisted that his surgery be performed on the Monday for which it had been originally scheduled, rather than on the Friday he was now being urged to accept because an opening in the schedule had occurred. First he said, "I'd rather wait until Monday." When the doctors pressed him, he said, "There's going to be no surgery until Monday." And there wasn't.

The times when you're not on a one-to-one basis with your doctor create a special problem. When you go to a hospital or visit a specialist, for example, other doctors are now involved in your life and they may use a different vocabulary or give different meanings to the same words. At such times you have a right to expect your own physician to be your advocate. He should furnish the hospital or specialist with a full report of your condition, and he should participate with you and the hospital or specialist in any decision concerning future treatment.

That takes work on your part as well as the doctor's. Sometimes your doctor won't know what's happening unless you keep him informed. Don't rely entirely on the specialist to do that. A patient of mine went to a urologist recommended by a friend to determine whether his bladder should be drained. The specialist decided that it should be, and informed the patient. The patient called me, quite upset, demanding to know why I hadn't informed him that his condition had changed. It hadn't changed. The question had simply been resolved, but the specialist had not done an adequate job of explaining to the patient, and he hadn't informed me at all. It was my fault for not staying on top of the matter; my patient could also have helped by demanding a clearer explanation, which he might then have relayed to me.

The doctor's explanations always need to be purified of jargon. Whether they're being given by your own physician or a specialist you've been referred to, you're the one who monitors them. The simplest way of getting your doctor to stop using jargon is to tell him, "I don't understand those words. Please put it in layman's language."

It's also important to understand that when you communicate with your doctor more than words are involved.

There are many forms of nonverbal communication—body language. One communicates by the way he looks, or the way he sits, what he does with his hands and eyes. A doctor's words can seem to be calm and reassuring, and yet the effect of his visit with a patient can be unnerving for reasons he's totally unaware of. I once had a patient with a liver problem serious enough to require hospital care. In the hospital one morning, as I tried to re-assure her that her condition was improving, she nonetheless seemed disturbed. Later I received a call from her sister asking what I'd done to disturb the woman. I protested that I'd simply reassured her that her jaundice had receded and that in all like-lihood her hospital stay would be shortened. And then it occurred to me what had happened. Just before visiting the patient I had learned that my mother had been hit by a truck and hospitalized with a broken hip. Obviously, I had carried my worry into my patient's room, and she had picked up on it, assuming that I was worried about her.

Patients also give clues. Women may hide behind their hairdos. Men may shield their eyes, or look away—mannerisms that are signs of anxiety. The anxious patient may also sit on the edge of his chair and lean on the doctor's desk. I have my own procedure for dealing with this kind of tension. I ask my patient to sit back, drop his hands and shake them, take a deep breath, and slowly exhale. My suggestion is usually met with a laugh—an indication the patient has at least recognized and accepted his tension.

If a patient is really uptight I may ask him to close his eyes and imagine he's on a beach, remind him what the sand feels like under his feet, how the fresh air smells, what the waves sound like. I try to convey that there's a world outside this doctor's office he can look forward to.

It's not too difficult to train yourself to think of a pleasant experience that will relax and help free you up for communication.

Another way to reduce tension is to reduce what you're going to say to as few lines as possible, and then rehearse just those lines. Suppose you intend to ask your doctor about getting another medical opinion on your case—and you're worried that he'll be angry. Figure out why you want the other opinion, and then make a little speech either to yourself or to someone close to you. It's better if you can rehearse with someone who can pretend he's the doctor and offer some predictable arguments.

The dialogue might go something like this:

YOU: I think I'd like to get another opinion.

YOUR DOCTOR: Well, I don't think it's necessary.

YOU: I'm a little uncomfortable.

YOUR DOCTOR: I've given you all the facts. I don't understand why you want another opinion. Why do you want one?

YOU: I'm the kind of person who doesn't like to take chances.

YOUR DOCTOR: There are no chances here. It's all been clearly outlined for you.

YOU: I'm just not willing to give that much power over my life to anyone. I ask for several opinions in anything important I do.

At this point, the doctor should accept your viewpoint. You haven't personally attacked him, or suggested that you don't trust him. All you've said is that you believe it's the intelligent thing to do.

Another way to reinforce your ability to communicate is to "model" on someone who is assertive and effectively advocates in his own interest. That person may have a way of sitting or standing or walking. When someone is assertive, his total demeanor begins to change. By studying such a person and imitating his look and gestures and manner, you can brace yourself for the time when your words will need to be firm.

Knowledge by itself is not enough. It must be presented with conviction, and without apology.

GIVE AND TAKE

As in most human relationships, you've got to give to get. As you leave the prison of awe and communicate freely with your doctor, your new expectations need to be balanced by an appreciation of the doctor's legitimate pressures.

Your doctor owes you a committed ear and a focused mind. If your visit is constantly being interrupted by phone calls, and the interruptions are affecting your ability to communicate, I suggest that you say so to your doctor. For example: "I'm finding it a little difficult to talk with these calls coming in. Is it possible to hold all but the emergency calls until we've finished? I promise I won't be long." There are four kinds of patients who compete for your doctor's time—the office patient, telephone patient, hospital patient, and house patient. You're the office patient at the moment, but next week you could be in another category, with needs that seem pressing to you. One of the more valuable results of my feedback sessions has been the increasing awareness my patients have gained of one another's needs. None of these qualifications, however, diminish the doctor's responsibility to focus his attention on you.

If you believe that your doctor's attention is wandering, tell him so. "Are you listening to me?" my patients have occasionally asked. Everything depends on how it's said. If it's said in anger, it doesn't work so well. If it's offered as an acknowledgment that I'm human too, it might even give us both a laugh and a moment of relief. Remember that the time may come when your doctor's mind may momentarily drift as he talks to another patient because he's thinking about you.

What can you do to make your doctor respond more to you?

You can make him feel good about the care he's rendering. Your doctor is paid for his care. But being a human being, he needs to be appreciated, not reverentially by some mute worshipper, but genuinely by a collaborator in a relationship. It's not just a question of saying, "Thanks for getting me well." It's the kind of gratitude that communicates your appreciation for having learned something about your body and your emotions that will keep you from becoming ill again in the same or similar fashion. What's even more gratifying to your doctor than curing your ulcer is hearing you say, "I know now that there are certain ways I've been handling my life that contributed to this ulcer, and I know how to prevent its recurrence."

A smart patient lets his doctor know if he's become better. Many times a patient will call late at night with a problem and I'll give him a suggestion and then not hear from him again for months. I have no way of being certain he's recovered. The next time he calls, he may say, "Well, I got better, and I didn't feel there was any need to call you." Put yourself in the doctor's position. Would you be satisfied? You don't have to speak directly to the doctor. You can leave a message with his secretary or answering service. That little gesture on your part may not be important in terms of specific treatment, but it prepares the way for better communication later on. And so for better long-range health care.

The final test of your ability to assert yourself with your doctor is your capacity to tell him that you're leaving him, and why.

Too often patients stay in unhappy relationships that dehumanize and hurt them. They do so for several reasons: Perhaps the doctor is located in their neighborhood, and it's convenient to see him. Or they're cynical about doctors in general, and don't believe a change of doctors will improve things. Or they hold the doctor in awe and are frightened of a change, lest the continuity of their care be interrupted.

There are times when a doctor-patient relationship just isn't going to work out. Either there are personality conflicts or else the patient has lost confidence in the doctor's abilities. Under such circumstances, it's unwise to continue the relationship. One evening at a feedback session a patient of mine said he'd wanted to leave me but felt he couldn't because his case was so complicated.

"I want you to understand," I said. "It's very important that you don't stay if you're unhappy." I told him that another physician could learn the details of his case, that I would send his records, and that a good physician would grasp the history and current situation. The patient left me for a doctor whose personality suited him better.

There is no situation so complicated that a patient should feel a doctor owns him.

In 1623, John Donne wrote this line in *Devotions:* "I observe the physician with the same diligence as he the disease." If you will do the same, and then communicate what you've learned to your doctor, your relationship can only prosper. Even if this communication sometimes causes pain of its own, it is at least therapeutic, a part of the process of *you* helping to make and keep you healthy.

COMMUNICATION HINTS

Tell your doctor when you don't understand.
Repeat what he tells you.
Write down what he tell you.
Ask him to repeat his instructions, either now or a few days later.
Ask about your choices.
Express your emotions honestly.
Take time to reflect.

Be firm about what you want.

Use relaxation techniques just before you speak.

Reduce what you want to say to as few lines as possible.

Rehearse what you intend to say.

Model on someone who is appropriately assertive.

6

Should You Obey Your Doctor?

NOT OBEY your doctor? That seems ridiculous. You're paying him for his advice, aren't you? He knows more than you, doesn't he? Nonetheless, innumerable studies show that patients routinely ignore their doctors' instructions. One study at the outpatient department of the University of Rochester School of Medicine demonstrated, in fact, that fifty-one percent of the patients did not even take the medicine that had been prescribed for them.

Researchers have tried to learn whether there's any pattern here. Are rich patients less likely to comply than poor ones? Does the level of noncompliance increase or decrease with the level of education? Several studies of such questions were reviewed in *The Journal of the American Medical Association* in 1974. None of the findings could attribute noncompliance primarily to social or cultural backgrounds.

It is reasonable, then, to suggest that the cause may be found in the relationship—or rather the lack of it—between doctors and patients.

THE ROOTS OF NONCOMPLIANCE

The first time I doscovered that a patient of mine hadn't followed through on my instructions, I became upset and told my concern to several older physicians. "Forget it," one of them said. "Patients aren't always going to do what you tell them. You're doing well if they follow even a part of your orders."

I remember vividly how he used the word "orders."

Consider, first, the word "compliance." It suggests an unequal, and psychologically unacceptable, relationship. It means that one party is giving orders and the other party is obeying orders, or is supposed to obey them.

I don't like the word "comply." I especially don't think you should "comply" with advice about which you may have some doubt. If you feel doubtful about the advice, that's reason enough not to comply until you've assured yourself of its wisdom by exploring your thinking with your physician.

Traditionally, medical studies explain noncompliance by suggesting that the patient is somehow deficient. It's your fault because you can't or won't follow through on the doctor's advice. Few suggest that perhaps you haven't been receiving the key element of understanding; few ask about the empathy and warmth of the doctor; few bring up your right to question and to change your mind based on the answer you receive from the doctor.

When you don't get an explanation, when you don't feel the doctor's warmth, when your expectations aren't fulfilled, when you don't receive the doctor's trust and confidence, you may not take the doctor's advice. The irony is that the medical mystique the doctor uses to shield himself defeats his efforts to heal.

A patient once came to me short of breath and feeling uncomfortable. Examination disclosed chronic, obstructive pulmonary disease, or emphysema. The patient, a department store executive, had been seeing a doctor with an excellent reputation. In taking his history, I learned he'd not continued with the medication his previous physician had prescribed. When I asked why, he gave me a perhaps oblique but nonetheless revealing answer. He'd found it difficult to question his previous doctor. The doctor would cut him off, make him feel uncomfortable. The result was he became so insecure about his relationship with his doctor he lost confidence in the prescribed treatment.

There's a strange contradiction here. Patients set up their doctors as gods. But they disobey what their gods tell them to do. It's analogous to religious people who say they believe in God but don't practice their faith. One reason they don't is that they may not understand it. Another reason is that they may find it alienating and threatening and even frightening.

In a medical setting such ambivalence can only create problems. Indecision invariably translates into inaction. The patient doesn't take his medicine, doesn't return for his checkup, and often doesn't get well.

In most relationships between doctors and patients, the doctor is active and the patient passive. And yet in the overwhelming number of instances, the doctor's paternalistic manner—"doctor knows best"—will only put you off. You are aware of what's happening. You have to be a clod or a stone not to realize that you're being treated in a paternalistic way. A few patients may accept it and love it. Others will do nothing but cower. Still others cease to hear the doctor. Some run away. And some die. Most patients want to get well. Some doctors, by their attitude, defeat this basic, healthy motivation.

People relate mostly to symptoms. Once the obvious signs of an illness pass, they tend to become lax in their attention to the disease. Tubercular patients, for example, often stop taking drugs when they start to feel better and to gain weight. But for a tuberculosis treatment to be absolutely certain, the medication needs to be taken for a year to a year and a half.

The reasoning of patients who stop taking drugs as soon as the symptoms of illness disappear is certainly understandable. They know, for example, that drugs can have side effects; rather than risk side effects they stop taking the drugs. But as important as it is for you to participate in your own care, you need to do it out of knowledge, not ignorance.

By ignorance I don't, of course, mean stupidity. I mean, very simply, lack of knowledge, which usually results from your neglecting to ask the doctor what you need to know, or the doctor neglecting to tell you, or you not understanding him and then not saying so and asking for clarification.

I once had a patient who wasn't responding as he should to the medication I'd prescribed for a kidney infection. We reviewed every detail of his treatment until I finally discovered he'd been taking his medication three times a day instead of the four I'd prescribed. When I asked him why, he said he would have to wake up at night for the fourth dose, and he didn't want to do that. I hadn't sufficiently impressed on him how important that fourth dose was.

It's been estimated that fifty percent of discovered cases of diabetes are inadequately treated because the patients stop taking their medication. When someone has a disease that's inadequately treated, it's as if the disease had never been discovered.

A MATTER OF MOTIVATION

If you have a high level of cholesterol in your blood, you can't work the level down and then simply return to your old eating habits. Yet patients do it all the time. I was visited by one man whose cholesterol level was two times the normal level. He was knowledgeable and highly motivated. For the next several months, at my suggestion, he stayed away from fatty foods, red meats, excessive dairy and delicatessen products. He also began to exercise. Gradually his cholesterol diminished until it was at an acceptable level. The next time I saw him, however, the level had significantly climbed. When I asked him why, he said that since the problem had been eliminated and he felt fine, he had begun to eat "normally" again. Normal for him, I said quickly, was the low-cholesterol diet for the rest of his life.

How you're feeling now is important now, but you have to consider what you're doing in terms of what it can mean for the future. Disease can take years to develop. It should be anticipated with a reasonable commitment to good health habits. But doctors who *order* you to adopt good health habits only alienate and discourage you from acting in your own best interests.

The question in your mind—whether implicit or expressed—is, "What's in it for me?" You judge medical care by whether or not it does the job. That seems to make sense, except that your understanding of what the "job" is may be faulty.

Too often physicians take an either/or attitude: Either you accept everything I say, or you're not following through. But advice must be made personal and relevant. If you're very sick, you'll usually do what you're advised to do. If you have a passing illness, or are being advised to adopt certain health habits to guard against disease, you may take the "it can't happen to me" attitude. Only when and if illness enters a certain type of patient's immediate universe—the death by cancer of a relative who smoked, for example—will he consider a change in habit. Otherwise, he tends to play roulette with his health.

The advice, therefore, that your doctor gives you must be so thorough that its logic is overpowering. I had one patient, an advertising executive, who drank heavily. He was not an alcoholic, but his drinking went well beyond the prudent level. He didn't want to stop; he enjoyed it, and besides, he argued, it was a tool of his trade. A Madison Avenue lunch, tradition held, began with a dry martini. To solidify his case, he read up on cirrhosis of the liver. He found that by eating something when he drank, and by taking vitamins, he could minimize the damage of alcohol. So he continued to drink confidently for two years—until his next examination indicated an enlarged liver, and chemistries suggested damage. What he had been unable to accept—and what I had not been able to impress on him—was that there is a great deal medicine doesn't yet know about what causes cirrhosis of the liver. He thought he'd covered all eventualities. Neither he, nor his doctor, knew enough to make that possible.

At the other extreme, there are people who believe they and everybody else should do as the doctor says, no matter what. A sixty-year-old man came to me in such poor condition that I put him on a rehabilitation program that excluded the three social drugs: caffeine, nicotine, and alcohol. In their place I prescribed a mild tranquilizer. But the pills made him sleepy. He stopped taking them— and told his daughter. *She* went into a rage. "For once in your life, you're going to do what the doctor tells you," she told her father. Yet the last thing I advocate is compliance with my advice *just* because I give it. Different people react differently to medication. They need to be encouraged—not discouraged—to observe their reaction and report it to their doctor.

THE GOAL—MUTUAL PARTICIPATION

The argument for mutual participation is overpowering. Example after example demonstrates that nonparticipation by the patient can be dangerous and participation beneficial.

In my own practice I prescribed a diuretic for a patient to reduce the amount of water in her system. But I did not sufficiently impress her with the knowledge that as her body adapted to the diuretic, she would not urinate as much as she had in the beginning. When, in fact, that happened, my patient, on her own, increased the dosage, assuming that she was supposed to continue urinating as she had at the outset. Over a period of several weeks she became very weak and developed hypokalemia, a condition of low blood potassium. Once we found out what was happening we were able to remedy the condition. And we agreed that the culprit was faulty communication. I hadn't sufficiently explained the medication and its expected side effects, and she hadn't asked the questions she'd wanted to ask.

I also treated a young diabetic who needed to calculate to the gram the amount of food he ate.

Not only did his food have to weigh an exact amount, it had to be eaten at an exact hour. He was intelligent, he understood the nature of his illness, the importance of controlling his blood sugar, and the complications that might occur if he didn't. Nonetheless, he kept reporting back with his blood sugar in a high, uncontrolled state. It developed that the schedule I'd put him on went cross-grain to his life style. It interfered with his school schedule, his sports, and his social life. Having to stop in the middle of a basketball game, for example, made him miserable and upset him. He felt like an invalid. In all likelihood the emotional upset had aggravated the very diabetes we were trying to treat. So we searched together for a solution to fit his life style. He figured out a way to coordinate his everyday life and his medication by periodically measuring at convenient times the amount of sugar in his urine and adjusting intake accordingly. Over the next several months his condition changed dramatically as his blood sugar stabilized in the normal range, and he felt his normal self instead of a perpetual patient.

There was *no way* that I, as his physician, could have worked out the treatment alone. I needed his help to get him better. He needed me. If we hadn't mutually participated in his cure, either his disease would still be uncontrolled or he would be resentfully following my original instructions and living a miserable life.

What I'm urging is a system in which the doctor trains you to care for yourself under his supervision. You become, in effect, the monitor of your own illness. A mystique doctor would say, "This patient is practicing medicine without a license." The humanistic doctor says, "This patient can be trained to participate actively and creatively in his own care."

Patients who have been encouraged to grapple with their own health problems have demonstrated remarkable creativity. On several occasions patients with high cholesterol have given me recipes they've invented to ease the transition from enticing but damaging foods to nourishing diets. I, in turn, have passed these recipes on to other patients with the same problem. Often, too, patients have reported back that they've found a more effective time to take a certain medication. The idea is to operate within the boundaries I've tried to establish with them, but to have enough room and flexibility to function on one's own with confidence.

MEDICATION IN PERSPECTIVE

We've become a drug-oriented society. Many physicians find it easy to give a prescription. You're nervous? Take tranquilizers. A respiratory infection? Here's a prescription for an antibiotic. But drugs don't deal with the basic problem. The don't go into *why* a patient is tense. They don't get at smoking or eating problems. They can't motivate a patient to exercise. And, as mentioned, drugs can have side effects. You owe it to yourself, therefore, to ask questions when medication is prescribed for you. You are entering into a new relationship with your doctor. Formerly, you rarely questioned what he told you. Now, you will. In order to get good answers, you have to ask good questions.

Ask what the medication is meant to do.

Ask what your condition should be two days hence, a week hence, three weeks hence.

Ask about possible side effects.

Ask whether the medication can be taken in conjunction with other medication.

Ask about prohibitions on food and drink in connection with your medication.

Ask about the length of time you should take the medication.

If the dosage is inconvenient, ask whether it can be modified.

Ask your doctor what his experience has been with the drug. Doctors may get their information from drug advertisements or pharmaceutical-house representations. That's because of the press of time, but it's not the ideal way. Information about drugs is best obtained from the medical literature, or from colleagues who've given the drug to patients. If you want further information about the drug your doctor prescribed, you can consult the *Physicians' Desk Reference (PDR)* to see what it has to say about side effects.

Vitamin B-12, for example, is a beautiful red-colored liquid. It's widely prescribed throughout the country for fatigue. It's excellent treatment for pernicious anemia or diabetic neuropathy, but most often it's given because patients want a lift. The trouble is that once such treatment starts, it can become habituating. Without it, the patient feels recurrently fatigued. And, more important, the treatment can obscure serious disease.

One of the best ways to help yourself to be the monitor of your own health is to bring a notebook to your visit with your doctor. Make comprehensive notes of what he suggests, what signs you should look for and, depending on which signs appear, what modifications to try after consulting with your doctor.

We're dealing now with potent drugs. They're marvelous drugs. They can do wonders for you. But they need to be handled well and adeptly, not only by the doctor but by you. There's one antiarrhythmic drug in particular whose dosage may vary with the pulse rate. The drug is used to treat angina. It slows the heart rate. The goal is to slow the rate to an acceptable level without slowing it too much. The pulse is the heart's signal. You can learn to take your pulse in a matter of minutes. One of my patients, suffering from angina, learned this simple procedure and was delighted with this minor exercise in demystification—matter of fact, when he felt his pulse, his face literally glowed. A week later he telephoned to tell me that his pulse was in the mid-fifties. I asked him to come to the office, where I verified his reading. We then reduced his medication. He still had relief from his angina, but his pulse increased to a safer level.

Another suggestion: bring your medication with you whenever you visit your doctor. That does several things. It gets rid of old bottles of medication that your doctor judges to be no longer relevant to your treatment. It establishes and doubly checks in your mind as well as in your doctor's that you're on the right course of treatment. And it cues you and your doctor to a thorough review of your overall treatment and health habits.

I also recommend that you ask your doctor to request that the pharmacist put an identifying description on the label of any prescription. The prescription itself should be typed out, if possible, but in any case it should specify that the drug is for shortness of breath, or palpitations, or whatever lay terminology describes your condition.

You should intervene in all the steps along the medical process. The pharmacist, too, is human, capable of errror. The pills he gives you can be the wrong ones. It happens. How often have you been unable to decipher a prescription you've carried to your pharmacist? If you have trouble reading it, it may be just as difficult for the pharmacist. Ask him.

It's important for you to question the pharmacist if you believe that the pills you're receiving differ in size or color or texture from those you've had before. It's important to ask if there's an alternative to a certain pill if it looks like another pill you're taking for other reasons. One of my patients came into the office in heart failure that was difficult to explain. It developed he'd mistaken some diabetic medication for his heart medicine and had interchanged the dosages.

Finally—and very important, however self-evident—the minute you feel worse or different than you expected to as a result of taking any medication, get in touch with your doctor.

GETTING ANOTHER OPINION

There's a moment of truth in your relationship with your doctor—when you tell him you'd like another opinion. You must have the courage to tell him, and he should welcome the request. Don't be afraid of angering your doctor.

Some of my patients will routinely want another opinion when it comes to any kind of surgery. Even when I show them something as obvious as gallstones on an X-ray, they'll still ask to see another doctor. I welcome the request. There are differences of opinion in medicine. There are controversies.

Some physicians will elect surgery for a situation; others will feel it's not indicated.

There are judgments involved in medicine. There's a certain amount of set technology from which decisions automatically flow. But there are other circumstances in which this isn't the case at all. Since it's understood there are differences among physicians about how to treat certain illnesses—the internist, for example, may look at things differently than a surgeon—it follows that it's reasonable to get additional opinions.

It may be difficult, even painful, the first time you try to appropriately assert yourself with your doctor. You may suffer a setback. You may jeopardize your relationship. Physicians are humans with egos. But the physician who's a reasonably secure human being won't feel shattered by your suggestion that you see another doctor; in fact, he will welcome it as a standard procedure and a patient's right. If your doctor can't tolerate, much less support, a more assertive behavior, it's reasonable for you to question whether he really is the right doctor for you.

The informed patient takes a stake in his treatment. He feels confident about monitoring his well-being. He expresses his doubts to his doctor, and he doesn't act until he has been convinced beyond a reasonable doubt that the course he's electing is the right one. He does all this together with his doctor.

Compliance is old-fashioned medicine. *Cooperation* is interim medicine. *Mutual participation* is modern medicine—being part of the patient-doctor team.

7

The Hospital

IS THIS TRIP
REALLY NECESSARY?

THERE ARE five basic questions to ask your
doctor before you consent to enter the hospital:

> Why am I going?
> What will be done?
> How long will I stay?
> What will it produce?
> What will happen if I don't go?

The reasons patients enter hospitals are about
evenly divided between nonsurgical and surgical.
Nonsurgical hospital visits are for observation and
treatment of the heart, lung, kidneys, gastrointestinal area, endocrine problems, and arthritis, or for

matters relating to pediatrics, neurology and dermatology.

The medical mystique has a special effect on surgical patients. The patient is going to be anesthetized and operated on. His life will literally be in the hands of a highly skilled surgeon during a brief period of time. He not only feels vulnerable. He feels awe.

Not all surgery, of course, requires hospitalization, but whenever a doctor indicates you need minor surgery that can be performed in the office, it's wise to do two things. First, ask whether it wouldn't be better to have the surgery performed in a hospital. Second, decline to have the surgery performed during the visit when it's suggested. Allow yourself time to consider, evaluate, and adjust.

While I believe that most surgery should be performed in a hospital, I'm not opposed to minor surgery in an office. I do feel, though, that a certain amount of emotional preparation is required, in any case.

You need an opportunity to reflect on what the doctor has recommended in order to give your informed consent. You'll be able to consider whether you have the emotional resources to have the surgery, and deal with your postoperative needs at home. I had a patient with a cyst in her breast whom I referred to a surgical specialist. He wanted to aspirate the fluid out of the cyst at the first office visit. She told him she wasn't in an emotional state to handle the procedure at that time. The surgeon responded to that by urging her to get another opinion; she did; it confirmed the first opinion. She then returned to the first surgeon, feeling very good about his sensitive response to her concern, and let him perform the surgery in his office.

The overriding question for you is whether surgery is necessary or whether there are alternate treatments that might be equally as good. To inform yourself fully, getting another opinion may be even more indicated than in the case of your primary-care physician or nonsurgical specialist discussed in the previous chapter. The intent in all instances isn't to shop around, it's to confirm a diagnosis and course of treatment. Judgments differ, especially in regard to elective surgery for gallbladder disease or hernia—not only whether, but when.

Suppose you get several opinions, all different. One doctor says surgery is necessary. A second says it should be put off for several months, pending new tests. A third says the condition can be cured by medication and won't ever require surgery. What can you do? How can you tell who's right?

All physicians vary in expertise, skill, and compassion. There's a variation in mortality and morbidity from hospital to hospital when comparing the same surgical procedure. Your primary-care physician can get an idea about who's good in a special field by calling members of his own hospital's staff and asking for recommendations. Surgeons he respects could furnish him the names of competent specialists in other fields.

The surgeon works with a team; a team can be highly experienced in particular areas of surgery— or, conversely, without much experience in those areas. A few straightforward questions may elicit the information: How many such operations has the surgeon done in the last year? How many were successful? What's the hospital surgical staff's experience with the operation?

You'll also want to know whether the surgeon whose service you're contemplating or whose advice you're seeking is "board-certified." Of the 92,600 practitioners who involve themselves in surgery, only about one-half, 45,600, are board-certified surgeons. There are 20,600 uncertified surgeons, 9,700 general practitioners who perform some form of surgery, and 15,800 surgical interns and residents. All may be competent, but only the board-certified surgeon has taken special training and passed certain standardized tests indicating his proficiency.

You can find out independently whether the surgeon to whom you've been referred is a certified specialist by writing the American College of Surgeons, 55 East Erie Street, Chicago, Illinois 60611. Your local medical society has a directory of medical specialists. Your library probably has one, too. Information about the hospital where the surgery is to be performed can be obtained from the Joint

Commission on Accreditation of Hospitals, 65 North Michigan Avenue, Chicago, Illinois 60611.

Let me repeat here for emphasis a point I made in an earlier chapter. I believe it is a serious mistake to go directly to a surgeon when you have a problem. He may be more inclined to think in terms of surgical solutions. He will not be as knowledgeable about you as your primary-care physician. Your physician can give you the names of several surgeons, whose backgrounds you can compare. You can then consult two or three of them.

All of the skills you've developed in diagnosing your primary-care physician should be employed in examining your prospective surgeon. Obviously, your expectations should be just as exacting in considering a surgeon as in considering your regular doctor. In addition, you'll want to ask certain specific questions of each surgeon you visit:

> At what hospital do you operate?
> How often do you perform this operation?
> What's been the result?
> Can you describe the operation?
> What are the risks?

The surgeon's thoroughness can tell you a great deal about him. A patient of mine contemplating open-heart surgery once visited two surgeons. The first listened to his heart with a stethoscope and opined—on the basis of my workup—that the surgery was necessary. The second did his own extensive examination to corroborate mine, and concluded, "You don't have a choice. You've got to have this operation. If you don't, you'll be dead in five years." *Then* the choice was a clear one.

When it isn't, and even though you've made your own informed investigations, it's wise to return to your primary-care physician, give him your impressions, and discuss the decision with him. Even if the choice already seems obvious, a final chat with your doctor is a good idea. He can give you another invaluable piece of information: ask him how often any of the surgeons whose names he's given you have indicated in previous referrals that surgery wasn't necessary. On numbers of occasions I've referred patients to a particular surgeon who specializes in treating nodules in the thyroid, only to have him recommend that a period of time elapse before a decision for surgery be made.

The last of those five basic questions is a critical one, and should be asked of both your primary physician and potential surgeon: What will happen if I don't have surgery?

The answer may be that you don't need it. A recent study in the *New England Journal of Medicine* (1974) by Dr. Eugene G. McCarthy and Geraldine W. Widmer gave this impressive statistic: twenty-four percent of surgical procedures recommended by surgeons were not confirmed by second opinions. In a percentage of those cases, the first surgeon may have been right, but it's obvious that there's a high percentage of cases in which disagreement exists and unnecessary surgery might occur. That alone should emphasize why a second opinion is important.

When you are considering surgery you will naturally be in an emotional state, inclined to revert to a greater dependency than in normal times. You may also be inclined to abdicate unpleasant decision-making to the doctor; it's imperative that you resist the desire to do so. You should not let your emotions make the decision. You should listen critically both to the surgeon recommending an operation and the one who says it's unnecessary. The reasoning of both of them should be so coherent that the options are clearly presented and you then know and understand the alternatives.

You should also take into account your own built-in predispositions. If, for example, your father died of cancer, you may be disposed, even eager, to have exploratory surgery at the first indication of a problem; or, conversely, you may tend to resist knowing anything at all. You'll need others around you to help put the problem in perspective, including family and friends—part of the lay-referral system—who amongst them may know other situations similar to yours.

Finally, though, you, with the aid and counsel of your primary-care physician, must make the choice.

HOW TO USE THE HOSPITAL

The patient who's learned to be appropriately assertive in his doctor's office can be equally effective in the hospital. He can ask intelligent questions that will earn him respect, improve his care, and conceivably shorten his stay. He can be an agent of change, aware of what's going to happen to him, monitoring his own progress.

The American view of hospitals is filled with puzzling contradictions. On the one hand there's an awareness of and admiration for the scientific competence of most hospitals and their achievements in saving lives. On the other hand there's an uncharitable view of hospitals as cold, inefficient, and expensive institutions that one enters with apprehension.

Even the statistics on attitudes toward hospitals are ambivalent. Some studies show that Americans are critical of the care they've received in hospitals. Other studies show that Americans believe they have received excellent hospital care.

Obviously, such widely different perceptions can only be accounted for by widely different experiences.

What accounts for the differences?

Some hospitals can, at times, embody all the flaws of the impersonal aspects of American medicine. A percentage of the problem is attributable to the shortage of money and the high cost of care. I have no competence to discuss the problems of hospital economics. Where I want to make a contribution, and believe I can, is in the area of the problem that exists in hospital care as a consequence of the medical mystique.

When you enter a hospital, you're extending and expanding your medical care. It now is dependent not on one doctor, or two, but on a network of hospital house physicians, nurses, aides, and technicians. Routines, rules, schedules, and procedures increase your feeling that you've been placed in a strange environment, removed from your familiar patterns.

And then, of course, you are sick, with all the apprehension that goes with it. If ever there were a time when you could benefit from sensitive concern, it's when you're in the hospital. Unfortunately such care isn't always forthcoming.

Some things that happen in the hospital may make you feel a loss of identity, make you feel as though you are only a case, not a person. You may be aware of an insistent rhythm of procedure that's difficult to interrupt. Your questions may not merely be unanswered, you may never get an opportunity even to ask them. You may overhear conversations filled with medical jargon that bewilder and frighten you. You know there are other sick people around you whose needs must also be attended to. If you're like most people, you'll probably react to all this by withdrawing into your shell and as a result may not get all the attention you need and are entitled to. You may do this without realizing it, because you're conditioned not to question the *hospital* mystique— a sort of subcategory of the medical mystique.

How can these hospital problems be overcome? How can you be made more comfortable psychologically? First, you must be better prepared for the experience; you must be educated to question— rather than succumb to—the hospital mystique.

GETTING A BED

Hospitals have three categories of admissions: elective, urgent, and emergency. Sometimes it may be a question of judgment about whether a case is an emergency or urgent; what one physician considers urgent another might call an emergency. In order for such judgments to be complete, they need to include your insight.

There are times when your doctor's hospital is so active he can't get you in immediately and you have to stay at home. If your condition worsens and you feel you must enter the hospital at once, you have every right to tell your doctor that you want to go to another hospital. I suggest this request should be made only if your condition, in your judgment, is truly urgent. It's simply more practical for your doctor—and so for you—when he's working at his own hospital. If your condition *is* very urgent, however, then you should not be locked into the notion that only *your* doctor functioning in *his* hospital will suit you.

Basically, it's your physician's responsibility to get you into a hospital. But it's your responsibility as his patient to say, "I'm sorry, I can't wait." If it's becoming more urgent, your doctor should want to know it. Not telling him because you're afraid you'll upset him, or because your demand might sound like criticism, is tantamount to risking your life. Your relationship with your doctor should be sufficiently comfortable for you to be able to ask for action. But comfortable or not, you must ask.

Somewhere in your community there's a bed, whether it's in a voluntary teaching hospital or a municipal teaching hospital. There comes a point in an illness when the disease dictates your course of action. There is no situation, moreover, in which your doctor cannot attend in consultation with another hospital's staff.

If you're expecting to enter the hospital, I recommend that you prepare yourself psychologically for the possibility that you may not go in on schedule. With such an awareness, you'll at least be pleasantly surprised if you do. The hospital can control its admissions only up to a point. Emergencies take precedence over elective procedures. Patients already in the hospital may stay longer than anticipated. Predicting hospital demand is not always possible or precise.

Most hospitals are happy to get patients in and out as quickly as they can. The sooner one patient gets out, the sooner there is an opening for another. They don't like patients to be occupying a bed when nothing is happening, needs have been met and others are waiting.

If you're entering the hospital for elective surgery, it's probably best to enter on a Sunday night, with your surgery scheduled for a Monday. Obviously, not everyone can follow such a schedule. Generally speaking, the earlier in the week you can enter the hospital, the better off you are. But if the only time you can get a bed is a Friday night, and you must have your surgery the following week, it's advisable to accept.

If you're going to the hospital with an urgent problem, then the sooner the better, whether it's a so-called "good day" or not. Contrary to public opinion, hospitals *do* function on weekends— taking chemistries, cardiograms, and X rays, and there are constant evaluations by house staffs.

BRING A FRIEND—AND AN ASSERTIVE ATTITUDE

Anyone who isn't well, or who is contemplating surgery, may not be his own best advocate. It's a good idea to bring someone with you to help you cope with the admitting-office procedures at some hospitals.

These mostly are matters of long waits and red tape as you establish the basis of payment, informing the hospital of your insurance coverage, and how you intend to pay your bill if you don't have coverage or if the coverage isn't adequate. My own hospital, University Hospital at the New York University Medical Center, has done much to speed up admitting procedures by sending patients forms to fill out before their arrival.

The question of private versus semiprivate accommodations is completely up to you. The choice of room has never made a difference in any case, to my knowledge. Some people feel better by themselves. Others are helped by the socialization that goes on in a semiprivate room.

Once you're in the hospital, the questions follow logically:

> What's happening tomorrow?
> What will the tests determine?
> What will each drug accomplish?

Each time there's a change in the medication, you should expect to be informed, preferably in advance.

The failure of hospitals and doctors to inform patients in advance of procedures, tests and treatments—when they will occur and what they're for—needlessly increases the patients' anxieties.

The house staff as well as your doctor should inform you about everything that's happening. If your own doctor isn't informing you, he isn't doing his job. You can help matters by writing down your questions as they come to you, then putting them to the house staff and your doctor. By all means, telephone your doctor at his office; if you call him from your home, there's certainly no reason why you shouldn't call him from the hospital.

When you enter the hospital you should be on guard against a tendency to regress to a childlike posture. All the dependencies are heightened, just as when you're trying to make a decision about treatment. The key to overcoming the understandable anxiety you're experiencing is to learn what's happening to you day in and day out. The best way to ensure yourself of information is to identify with people in the hospital who are responsive and compassionate, and then to develop a relationship with these people. There's nothing mystical about this procedure. You've made friends all your life, and now you're making more. Just as you gravitate toward certain people on the outside, you'll be drawn to one or more persons on the hospital staff, whether a nurse or intern or resident. Express yourself to these people. Tell them about your doubts and worries and fears. Tell them you want to learn so you'll be able to give an informed appraisal of your reaction to medication or other care. The hospital personnel can't help but respect that attitude.

Often in the hospital the medical mystique has a very particular effect; it leads you to invest the personnel with more power than they actually have. You may cower when a little knowledgeable firmness will get you what you need.

One of the things you should know when you go into the hospital is that its staff has probably known your doctor over a period of years and has an understanding of his priorities and concerns. In this relationship, the hospital staff functions as the doctor's ally in the treatment of his patients. Presumably all patients will get as a matter of routine their pills and their meals and other necessary attentions. But there's a special concern and consideration that a staff can give whether in the office or at the hospital. Time and again, hospital nurses I've worked with have intervened with my patients to comfort them and correct misunderstandings that were disturbing them.

The best care in the world is available in teaching hospitals. You're examined three, four times by a different doctor each time. Some patients are bothered by this duplication, but it's really to their benefit; the doctors confirm one another's findings, as well as those of the primary-care physicians. If anything happens to you while you're in the hospital, the house staff will treat it immediately. One of my patients began to bleed internally while he was in the hospital—a fact that was revealed by his stool and confirmed by tests. One young house physician discovered that the patient had been taking an antacid to help his indigestion. This particular antacid contained aspirin, which the patient had been warned not to take.

I've also had patients who've had heart arrests in the hospital and were saved from death by the house staff.

Your doctor, of course, is your ally during all your stay in the hospital. His visits should be used to tell you everything that will be happening to you. But when he isn't immediately available you need to be able to act in your own interest.

It's true in the hospital, as it is outside, that the squeaking wheel gets the grease. But there is a difference between being aggressive and being assertive. The aggressive person will find himself being treated coolly. The assertive person who accurately describes his condition and needs will get attention and respect.

Most patients don't want to be known as complainers. They feel they must do everything possible to stay on the good side of the hospital personnel, even if it means not expressing their feelings. The irony is that time and again, those patients who appropriately assert themselves and speak up get the most attention from the hospital staff.

MAKING THE SYSTEM WORK FOR YOU

It's one thing to want to be assertive. It's another to remain physically and emotionally able to be so.

Ask your doctor whether it's really necessary for you to stay in bed. People in hospitals have a tendency to resign themselves to bed rest. Unless you're seriously ill, and specifically require bed rest, it's not so good a thing for you. Bed rest beyond eight hours is debilitating. Your body processes slow down, circulation becomes sluggish, the muscles become flaccid, your metabolism is lowered. I try to get my patients out of bed during the day, if possible—it helps make them feel life is going on.

There are also medical benefits to be gained by mobility. Spending time in a chair or on your feet reduces the possibility of blood clots forming in your legs. Getting out of bed also can lessen your anxiety.

Some of what happens to you when you enter the hospital that deprives you of identity and cuts you off from what's familiar and comfortable may be necessary, but at least some of it can be questioned.

Hospitals often require, for example, that you take off all your clothes and put on hospital pajamas and robe. It might help your morale if you were at least entitled to bring your own lounge clothes to the hospital.

Serving meals offers another example of a hospital procedure that may isolate you. Meals are invariably taken alone, at or near your bed. The food is unfamiliar. Maybe it could be served in a more congenial manner. The rest of the hospital would do well to study the therapeutic procedures often employed on the psychiatric floor. There, during the day, ambulatory patients wear their own clothes, and meals tend to be a social occasion in a large recreation area. They have a right to eat in their own rooms if they prefer, but they're encouraged not to. Patients on regular floors could be given the same option. Critically ill patients obviously couldn't participate, at least until they've recovered, but those medically able to take their meals together might welcome this opportunity to make friends and compare notes, making the hospital experience a little less intimidating.

Hospitals by their very nature are concerned with the delivery of care to large groups of people, and therefore are governed by such formidable matters as schedule constraints, utilization of facilities, and staff needs, as much as by patients' needs. The result is that hospital procedures may be inflexible and on occasion may seem insensitive to patients' feelings. In many hospitals patients are moved by wheelchairs or even stretchers to various laboratories, although they might be ambulatory. On paper it's a prudent measure, but it doesn't always consider each patient separately. The patient who can walk may be made to feel more helpless than he should; obviously such a feeling isn't very helpful for his general condition.

There needs to be more awareness by hospital staffs about what such things can do to patients' feelings about disease. The agent of change is the informed patient, standing up for his rights. He may not change hospital policy, but he can alert the hospital staff to *his* needs.

The cure for the hospital mystique—as for the overall medical mystique—is knowledge. On your part, knowledge of your own condition. On the house physician's part, knowledge of you, your family, your concerns. If illness isn't exclusively a physical phenomenon, the house doctor, no less than the family doctor, must be aware of your emotional makeup.

Hospital house physicians aren't consistently available for visits with the families of patients. They ought to find time. Some kind of schedule ought to be worked out to give the house physicians —and if not them, a social worker, or health educator—the opportunity to meet with the patient's family. Not to do so is to deprive physicians and their patients of potentially vital clues.

Some doctors will say there isn't time to do all this—you're in the hospital for diagnosis and treatment. But if you don't know a patient's feelings, you can't really know what's wrong with him. There's a direct relationship between healing and a patient's perception of how his physician regards and treats him.

Doctors have academic conferences on liver disease, heart disease, arthritis, and numerous other medical problems. There are currently no conferences on the techniques of communication, motivation, and education. There ought to be.

The great problem with hospital training is that it concentrates on the immediate problem—the diagnosis of a disease and recovery of the patient—and pays little attention to the illness in the context of your life. I remember how pleased the staff at my hospital and I were when a patient of mine recovered from congestive heart failure after several rough weeks. As she was being discharged, however, a social worker and a nurse came forward to say they were worried that the woman wouldn't be able to cope with the diet I'd outlined. Her condition required a low-salt diet, but she happened to love and crave pickles and smoked salmon—both high in salt. This was a sort of far-out situation, but it was real enough in this specific case. I resolved matters by suggesting the lady cook with garlic, onions, herbs, and spices other than salt.

Certain kinds of deprivation—especially the

apparently exotic ones such as indicated above—
may seem slight to doctors but they are difficult
for patients. And without the knowledge of such
idiosyncracies, doctors can't fully treat their patients.

When patients can't communicate with the hospital staff, they turn to one another. I've talked
about the "lay-referral" network common outside
the hospital. The network has its active counter-
part in the hospital. Sometimes it reduces to gossip,
with negative results. One evening a few years ago,
I visited a patient of mine who was in the hospital
for abdominal surgery and found her upset. During the day another patient had told her that the
surgeon who was to operate on her specialized in
cancer cases. This wasn't true; the doctor did other
kinds of surgery, and my patient didn't have
cancer. She had a benign polyp. But rumor had
convinced her that she had a fatal illness.

The lay-referral system needs to be institution-
alized. Instead of relying on casual meetings in
the hall, patients should have a place where they
can sit together with staff and communicate their
experiences. Encounters such as this will produce
less gossip, replace wrong information with facts,
and give patients an opportunity to relieve anxieties.

A hospital is a marvelous place for encounters
with patients who are experiencing the same problems as yourself. One elderly woman I know was
convinced she'd be a burden after surgery for an

artificial hip—until her orthopedist introduced her to other patients who'd had the same surgery and were walking.

In some hospitals, including my own, regular meetings of patients with a social worker as ombudsman are set up. Beth Israel Hospital in Boston has arranged for an in-house number for patients' complaints and suggestions. The patient simply dials CARE to talk about the food, the ventilation, etc.

Saturday morning is a relatively quiet time in the hospital. It would be an excellent time for representatives from the hospital's staff to meet with interested patients to discuss complaints and requests. Numerous hospitals currently give patients questionnaires on which they can record impressions. But such a procedure can't bring out the feelings behind these ideas the way a human encounter can. Moreover, the ideas come out while the problems in question are actually having their effect.

Happily there's a new kind of medical worker in the hospital today: the patients' representative. There are more than two million people working in the health-services industry, and of these *only some six hundred* are patients' representatives. Their job is to facilitate good treatment and care of patients in the hospitals. They provide a specific channel patients can use to look for solutions to their problems, worries, and special needs. They function as the patients' advocate. At New York University Hospital, a patient representative introduces herself to each patient admitted. She makes daily rounds, seeing the patients who have complaints about excessive noise, food, TV, other patients, bed pans, or anything else.

In one forty-five-minute period, according to an account in the magazine *Hospital Practice,* a patients' representative in the general-care division of Long Island Jewish–Hillside Medical Center in Queens, N.Y., counseled a nurse about how to encourage a teen-age girl with serious skin problems to keep a doctor's appointment that frightened her; discovered and reported that six pediatric patients were waiting for treatment but none was available; found an emergency staff overwhelmed with work and called for help; mothered a little boy; reunited a husband with his wife, who had been waiting on a stretcher just around the corner; put a mother in contact with her regular pediatrician for treatment of her child's broken nose; found a doctor for a woman with a severe back pain who'd been waiting for hours.

Much of the representative's work is simply communication—letting families and patients know about hospital policy and the reasons behind it, and offering counsel.

If the hospital you're treated in doesn't have a patients' representative, you'd be serving everyone by recommending such a person be hired.

Remember: hospital quality suffers badly without patient input. You're the patient. It's your input. Also your life.

KNOW YOUR RIGHTS

Hospitals perform necessary and valuable functions that must be carried out in an institutional setting. Unfortunately institutions tend to become depersonalized. Your problem as a patient is to express your individual needs and your rights until the time when hospitals develop procedures and training for better communication with you.

One of the best documents to be written in medicine in recent years is the "Patient's Bill of Rights," formulated by the American Hospital Association. It's a comprehensive statement that the prospective hospital patient ought to read before entering, and reread once there:

1. The patient has the right to considerate and respectful care.

2. The patient has the right to obtain from his physician complete current information concerning his diagnosis, treatment, and prognosis in terms the patient can be reasonably expected to understand. When it is not medically advisable to give such information to the patient, the

information should be made available to an appropriate person in his behalf. He has the right to know, by name, the physician responsible for coordinating his care.

3. The patient has the right to receive from his physician information necessary to give informed consent prior to the start of any procedure and/or treatment. Except in emergencies, such information for informed consent should include but not necessarily be limited to the specific procedure and/or treatment, the medically significant risks involved, and the probable duration of incapacitation. Where medically significant alternatives for care or treatment exist, or when the patient requests information concerning medical alternatives, the patient has the right to such information. The patient also has the right to know the name of the person responsible for procedures and/or treatment.

4. The patient has the right to refuse treatment to the extent permitted by law and to be informed of the medical consequences of his action.

5. The patient has the right to every consideration of privacy concerning his own medical care program. Case discussion, consultation, examination and treatment

are confidential and should be conducted discreetly. Those not directly involved in his care must have the permission of the patient to be present.

6. The patient has the right to expect that all communications and records pertaining to his care should be treated as confidential.

7. The patient has the right to expect that within its capacity a hospital must make reasonable response to the request of a patient for services. The hospital must provide evaluation, service, and/or referral as indicated by the urgency of the case. When medically permissible, a patient may be transferred to another facility only after he has received complete information and explanation concerning the needs for and alternatives to such a transfer. The institution to which the patient is to be transferred must first have accepted the patient for transfer.

8. The patient has the right to obtain information as to any relationship of his hospital to other health care and educational institutions insofar as his care is concerned. The patient has the right to obtain information as to the existence of any professional relationships among individuals, by name, who are treating him.

9. The patient has the right to be advised if the hospital proposes to engage in or perform human experimentation affecting his care or treatment. The patient has the right to refuse to participate in such research projects.

10. The patient has the right to expect reasonable continuity of care. He has the right to know in advance what appointment times and physicians are available and where. The patient has the right to expect that the hospital will provide a mechanism whereby he is informed by his physician or a delegate of the physician of the patient's continuing health care requirements following discharge.

11. The patient has the right to examine and receive an explanation of his bill regardless of source of payment.

12. The patient has the right to know what hospital rules and regulations apply to his conduct as a patient.

WHAT *YOU* CAN DO IN THE HOSPITAL

Be properly assertive and questioning.
Feel free to call personal family physician at appropriate time if there are any questions,

problems, upsets or anxieties; or have family or friend call.

Make written notes of questions, doubts, suggestions that you will want your primary-care physician to deal with.

Do same with house staff; ask them to stay as long as required, to sit, to amplify until you understand.

Read about your disease.

Ask for information about medication received.

Note any change in medication and inquire why.

Ask if your diet is appropriate.

Note which blood tests and why. Ask for results.

Note which procedures scheduled and why. Ask for results.

Become familiar with staff.

Know priorities of care.

Express your feelings, but try not to be aggressive.

Be your *own* best advocate. Be knowing about your condition and treatment.

If things aren't going according to your expectations, say so. Be direct, but not provocative.

Bring your own gowns, robes, lounge clothes if permitted.

Use leisure time to relax.

Eat in a chair if possible.

If medically permissible, be ambulatory, walk, sit, talk, socialize.

Be pleasantly, but persistently, assertive in terms of noise, other patients' disruptions, amenities, food, position in bed, ventilation in room, smoking.

Use convalescent facilities.

Conserve your resources, rest frequently.

Encourage cheerful visitors; tactfully ask others not to stretch their stay.

Learn to use the patient representative in hospital.

Be yourself.

8

Feedback

‑‑‑

"I FEEL you've been insensitive."

That statement from a patient would upset a doctor even if made in private. It had just been made by one of my patients with five other patients listening.

Before starting my feedback sessions I'd taken courses in group dynamics and spoken to numbers of knowledgeable people in the hope of learning how to make the sessions productive. Their advice to me was to listen, listen, listen, and interrupt as infrequently as possible. If any personal criticism were leveled at me, I was to take it without judgment or defense, I was to indicate by my silence and expression that it was acceptable for my patients to express their feelings—even if they were critical of their doctor.

Now, two years and more than fifty sessions later, we were seated in the waiting room of my office, and all eyes were on a woman in her mid-forties who'd just openly criticized me. As I studied her for a moment, I could feel my patients' looks shifting to me. When I looked at them, a few looked away. Others fidgeted. "I don't agree with you," another woman said quietly to the speaker. "I think Dr. Belsky's extremely sensitive—"

I held up a hand. "Wait a minute," I said. "We'll each have our turn. Let's at least try to be receptive to each other's feelings and experiences."

Again we looked to the original speaker. Three months earlier she'd had a lobectomy—a portion of the lung was removed. "I've been terribly depressed," she said, "and I don't think you noticed."

"I did notice," I said, "but I obviously didn't sufficiently show *you* that I had. That's not an excuse. If I've made you uncomfortable, I'm sorry."

The woman nodded. And then, almost imperceptibly, she smiled with relief. Not only had she spoken out and not been rebuked, she'd gotten something off her mind. She'd spoken up and would live to tell the tale.

I smiled too. The major aim of my practice—aside from the obvious one of healing—has been to put my patients on an equal basis with me, to help them see me as a person they can openly talk to. Here was solid evidence that it was happening.

Feedback encounters were not designed to be

gripe sessions or confessionals, but rather learning sessions in which patients could interact with their doctor and with one another and in the process enhance their chances for better health care. Patients' expectations and understanding of their responsibilities are interchanged and heightened. They come to see that as long as they acquiesce, as long as they are passive, as long as they're uninformed, as long as they don't care, they'll continue to be in a flawed relationship. Which literally isn't healthy.

There's usually little interpersonal feedback in the day-to-day relationship between a doctor and patient. The doctor rarely tells you how he feels about the way the two of you are interacting. You probably don't rush to the phone to report you're feeling better. The best indication of your satisfaction or feelings a doctor is likely to get is a neutral one: you keep seeing him. He submits a bill. It's paid. But even that isn't a reliable guide. There are patients who go on seeing a doctor they're not satisfied with—either because they're in awe of him or are afraid of the consequences of leaving, or simply because they want to avoid the hassle of finding another doctor. And there are, of course, negative feedbacks, the most extreme being malpractice suits or formal complaints to the county medical society—loud and clear signs of tremendous anger and rupture in the relationship. (We'll talk some more about malpractice suits in chapter 10.)

Whether they are negative or neutral, feedbacks normally available to a doctor are limited and often presumptive.

The feedback sessions I've held since 1973 originated out of my belief that I could do better. I suspected I was missing a good deal of information about the way my patients felt about me and the treatment they were getting. These feelings were important to the quality of medical care I was giving.

Most of what doctors learn has to do with disease. It's critical knowledge, of course. But we rarely spend any significant time on how to project new ideas to people or to motivate them. Still, that's exactly what I believe we must do when we apply our knowledge in practice.

Medical literature is filled with commentary about the poor state of patient-doctor communication, as well as exhortations that it be improved. Yet, nowhere does anyone suggest the use of feedback meetings between family practitioners and their patients.

The basic need in the social area of medicine is for the patient to know more about his doctor, and the doctor to know more about his patient. As I've said—and I think it bears repeating for emphasis—to accomplish this you need a new awareness of yourself and the ability to present it to your doctor. On his part, there's got to be a willingness to leave off from the medical mystiques and meet you face-to-face as a fellow human being. How can two people achieve this? There's only so much each can do alone. It isn't easy to change behavior. I think the process of change is helped along by group discussion, and that's what I designed my feedback sessions for.

Invitations to them are usually extended by me at the time of the patient's office visit. "Part of my approach," I say, "is to meet regularly with my patients. We talk about your experiences with doctors, your feelings about them and what you expect of them. We talk about what patients should be like—any topic or reaction, really, that occurs to you as a result of your involvement with me."

The patient's usual response is a sort of double-take "What?" After the initial surprise, most accept enthusiastically with something to the effect of, "Well, *that* will certainly be a new experience." Of those who don't accept some find the meeting inconvenient, or perhaps find the idea too new and threatening. They'd apparently rather hold onto their old feelings about doctors. Some patients, men mostly, say they want competent treatment and nothing more, thank you. They don't want to "get involved." Some patients assume I'm inviting them to a kind of group psychotherapy session, and they don't want that. I try to point out that the purpose of the meeting is for them to get experience that will help them get the best medical care. The feedback isn't designed to put anybody on the spot.

There's an important psychological corollary, I think, to this procedure. If people get to know you better, they may come to like you more and find it easier to understand your feelings and expectations. There's the chance, of course, that in knowing you better they'll like you less, but that's a chance one takes in any relationship. While the feedback sessions are primarily for the benefit of my patients, I too have certainly benefited. They give my patients a chance to know me—and it's then more possible to build our medical relationship on a basis of trust and, hopefully, even affection.

If the doctor is a real person talking about his own habits, about the ache he feels when he exercises or how tough it was to stop smoking, he provides a model of openness for his patients. My relationship with my patients has to be one in which I commit myself. They have to know that I'm not a hidden person, I'm not a mystery or a secret, I'm not shrouded in the mystique. The only way I know to convey that is through dialogue in a setting that promotes open discussion.

The size and makeup of the feedback sessions were carefully considered. I wanted a group small enough so that nobody felt overwhelmed by numbers. I wanted different personalities who would promote interaction in each group and encourage speaking up. At the same time I wanted to be sure the group wouldn't be monopolized by wordy talkers. Finally I wanted a varied group—old and young, those who'd been seriously ill and those who'd been more fortunate, those who'd been in hospitals and those who hadn't.

My objective, once the session is under way, is to keep the mood informal. No white coat, tie loose, collar unbuttoned. You can sense the old mystique is still very much present—the patients still look to me to lead, to be in charge. But my only "leadership" is to ask questions:

> What do you feel makes a good doctor?
> How do you feel about me as your doctor?
> What do you feel is a good examination?
> How do you judge competence?
> What would you do in an emergency?
> Suppose you were in a foreign city? How would you find a good doctor?
> Have I informed you well enough about your illness?
> Is anything wrong with my office procedures?
> Have the specialists I've referred you to been acceptable to you?
> What do you feel makes a good patient?
> How can I help motivate you?
> How do you get your health information? What does it mean to you, and what do you do with it?

These are some of the basic questions. Others naturally come up once the session is under way.

As each topic comes up I encourage the patients to talk it out among themselves; they may ask for my viewpoint but I avoid the request. I wait until they've finished with the discussion. The free interchange encourages them to say things they'd probably never tell me—or tell one another alone, for that matter. It's only at the end that I offer information or interpretation in an attempt to correct any factual errors or distortions, and to share my feelings.

Husbands and wives who come to the feedbacks together often bring up subjects they might not have confronted by themselves.

One evening we were discussing terminal illness. Did the patients want to be informed, or not? "If you're going to tell my wife she has cancer, I want to be told first," a husband said.

"Why do you want to know first?" his wife demanded.

"So I can figure out how to help tell you and prepare you."

She frowned. "I wouldn't want to be protected," she said. "I'd rather be told straightaway."

The same subject arose later at another feedback session. This one, too, involved a husband and wife. Here the wife said she preferred to know in advance if her husband had cancer, so that she could help him adjust. She hesitated. "And I may have to, if you don't stop smoking," she said softly. Her husband flushed. A few weeks later, he stopped smoking for good.

One of the few rules I follow in this interchange is never to reveal or give the slightest hint of the patients' medical condition. The patients, however, often volunteer details of their illness that seem appropriate to the discussion, even on such personal matters as venereal disease.

Each session differs, but one interchange seems characteristic of them all. It comes when I ask, "What's a good patient?"

"A good patient is someone who obeys his doctor," someone will invariably say. And the others tend to nod their heads.

"Suppose your doctor gives you medicine that makes you dizzy?" I may ask. "Would you continue to take it?"

"Of course not," someone will say.

"But if you don't take the medicine, you're not obeying the doctor."

The point is obvious, and the effect is sharp.

At the outset of each session, the patients are somewhat reluctant to criticize their doctor. They're wary of me and the group. To speak critically they've got to work their way through a lifetime of reverence. Almost invariably they start off by talking about other doctors. They almost never start with me. Positive feelings—being more acceptable—come first, preparing the way for any negative ones.

A function of a feedback session is to identify what's wrong and encourage constructive change. First we try to develop the ideal, then compare it to reality. The total reality usually contains positive elements that can be noted. But not to explore the negative ones in the context of the positive is to defeat the purpose of the sessions.

Many patients, for example, say their doctors are warm, compassionate people. Some, though, are bitter about past experiences. Young women often mention how they've been put into the stirrups of an examining table without so much as a hello. From this we try to talk out and discover why some doctors have trouble relating to their patients as human beings and what the patients should do about it.

The first and prime fact that emerges from feedback sessions is the awe so many patients feel for their doctors. One patient said he'd actually lied to his previous doctor about his condition because he was afraid if the doctor learned about his illness he'd probably bawl him out and he just wouldn't be able to cope with that. Another patient, who moments earlier had said that the most important characteristic of a good patient was to be honest with his doctor, said, "I've been honest with my doctors. But I haven't been open with them."

As the session progresses, patients begin to see they're capable of applying valid measures of a doctor's competence. Their observations become keener, bolder, more perceptive. Now some negative experiences begin to mix in with the positive ones: the patient who followed his doctor's instructions, only to develop an addiction; the patient whose mother was told by her physician he could only promise her a 50-50 chance of being cured of a complicated hernia, then learned from other doctors she didn't need the surgery; the patient whose father went into the hospital for a checkup, was diagnosed as an alcoholic but had never had a drink in his life. Such stories point up to the patients that doctors are fallible humans, and that patients must constantly be alert to normal errors as well as to those that arise out of incompetence.

Specialists tend to come up prominently in feedbacks. Some patients criticized a few of the specialists I'd sent them to. Either they felt that they'd been treated as though they were on an assembly line, or the doctor and/or his gatekeepers had been impersonal and abrupt, or they hadn't been fully informed about their illness. When two patients discover at a feedback that they've had opposite experiences with the same specialist, then they begin to see that what happens in a relationship has a lot to do with what they bring to it. And as the discussion proceeds, they often recognize in one another's remarks that they *do* have a capacity to judge the quality of their treatment.

The most bitter patient was a woman who'd been

referred to me by an internist I'd gone to medical school with. The woman's son had a congenital heart condition, which was being treated by a pediatrician. The doctor's manner convinced her he actually disliked children. Each visit was an ordeal, and she'd depart with her emotions spent. At one point she took her son to another doctor. But it was evident that this second doctor didn't have the competence of the first one. So she returned to the first doctor, who treated her son "successfully" at great emotional cost to mother and child.

The story I found most distressing was told by a patient who had been treated for hemorrhoids by a proctologist in a suburban community. Each time the woman returned to the doctor's office for the postoperative care she'd be placed in a "rectal" position, with her face down and her buttocks in the air. During one examination she said to the doctor, "You never see my face. How would you recognize me in a restaurant?"

"I'd ask you to turn around, bend over, and lift up your dress. Then I'd recognize you." A tasteless attempt at humor—and a devastating commentary on the negative aspect of the medical mystique.

There comes a time in each feedback session when my patients are ready to look critically at me. If criticism hasn't been expressed by this time, I encourage it. I offer criticisms that were noted at other feedback sessions. If this fails to cue them, I ask directly. When, for example, a patient mentions he was rushed by another doctor, I ask, "Have *I* been like that?" There'll be a certain amount of waffling until finally someone in the group will say that, yes, he did feel annoyed when he had to wait an hour to see me. Taking his lead, the other patients see that it's safe to be frank about their feelings and experiences and they begin to open up.

"You referred my mother to a psychiatrist and he gave her a drug that made her so sick she had to be detoxified in a hospital," a patient who had been with me for years blurted out one evening.

"I don't remember that," I said. "When was that?"

"Eight years ago," the woman replied.

"Eight years ago—and you never told me how you felt about it?"

"I couldn't."

"Why not?"

"Because I trusted you. I liked you very much. You know that."

I shook my head. "If you trust and like me, that's all the more reason why you should tell me. Our good feelings for one another will help us deal with the bad ones."

Another patient, this one a stockbroker:

"I think you're pretty inconsistent at times."

"How's that?"

"When I first came to see you, you gave me a

thorough physical and went into my health habits in detail. That was three years ago. I've seen you five times since then—"

"And I haven't asked about your health habits?"

"A couple of times. But not every time."

"Were there some that were bothering you?"

"Yes."

"Then why didn't you tell me?"

"I was waiting for you to ask."

I might have said we were both at fault in this case—me for not asking, he for not volunteering. Instead, I took the episode as another illustration of the inadequacy of communication between doctor and patient under normal circumstances, and a valuable feedback lesson. My patient had reminded me that there's a tendency to relax with patients who are familiar to you. I do ask all my patients about smoking and drinking at every meeting, but apparently I hadn't been asking year in and year out about the quality of his sex life or satisfaction at work. Patterns change as people age. It's my duty to keep informed. It's also the patient's duty to inform me, but I need to be alert in case he fails.

Another patient reminded me that I'd once had to answer the telephone while doing a proctoscopic examination on him. I joined in the sympathetic laughter, but I also felt discomfort— I'm sure not as bad as that patient's—and swore it would never happen again. It hasn't.

Still another patient, a young man who'd come to me for treatment of an acute liver condition brought on by excessive drinking, complained about the daily tranquilizer dose I'd prescribed to help him through his withdrawal.

"That stuff's making mashed potatoes of my brains," he complained at a feedback one evening.

"Then you should call and tell me," I said. My remark set off a chorus.

"Doctors are too busy," an older woman offered.

"When I'm talking to the doctor, I'm too nervous to ask the questions I mean to ask," a young secretary said.

"Doctors generally tend to overprescribe tranquilizers," a man in his thirties with a background in pharmacy offered.

They all looked at me. I raised my hands and shrugged. "You see? A smart patient begins to evaluate for himself the medication he's taking. He gives the doctor feedback. He says, 'Look, I don't want to take that much!' "

The feedback session isn't primarily about fallibility; criticism is often constructive. The *net* feeling has been a mix of regard, affection and confidence—cement to hold together our relationship and forgive me my lack of godliness.

For every upset, there are many warm moments. Patients will tell how they've used at critical periods what they've learned during office visits. One patient thought about the beach and water and sun while being rushed to the hospital with chest pains (applying my simple exercise in imagery that I recommend for getting some relief from situations of stress and pain). Another man, in the recovery room, turned his mind to a tennis match, calmed his anxiety, and helped his condition. The patients listening to these stories learned what they might do during similar emergencies.

There's been other healthy fallout. A young woman, listening to our discussion about how backgrounds affect response to symptoms, offered that she'd been modeling on her mother's behavior without realizing it. Her mother hadn't come for checkups; the daughter had followed her example. . . . A journalist discovered during a feedback session that the palpitations he'd been having were the result of caffeine in the large quantities of soda pop he'd been drinking just before retiring. . . . And there was a woman with a weight problem who acknowledged during a feedback session something she'd been unwilling to admit during consulation—that she'd been on a crash diet. "I guess I should have said this before and not been embarrassed," she said. "And how!" I said. Privately, later, I explained that this might be the clue to the elevated level of uric acid in her blood.

When these people voiced their feelings they were expressed not with bitterness or recrimination but mostly with affection and honesty. The complaints and misunderstandings, and even the compliments at the feedback sessions, have produced some changes in my practice that might otherwise never have occurred.

Since the start of these sessions, patients have remarked that I seem to listen differently and hear more. They also feel I show more concern.

I've learned that I speak too fast for some patients to understand me. I've tried to slow down.

I know now that as much as I abhor jargon, it sometimes creeps into my consultations, and I must constantly ask my patients if they've understood me, or to warn me if I'm talking medical lingo. With my patients' permission, I've taped several days in my practice, and then played it back. I was startled at how much jargon I did use, and how often I sounded rushed or abrupt.

I know better than to walk into an examining or hospital room without pausing to consider what expression I'm carrying in with me.

Some patients have been critical of me because occasionally reports weren't prompt. When I explained the circumstances to one patient, he said, "Well, if you'd only told me . . ."

"Right—and if you'd only asked me . . ." I'd assumed that he would conclude no news was good news—and that my chief concern was that nothing was wrong. I'd then neglected to put myself in *his* place, waiting for the results. And he had neglected to speak up for himself. We both learned something that otherwise might never have come up.

I know that patients are anxious when a test must be repeated. How to reassure them? I posed that problem to one of my feedback groups. They suggested some apropriate and less threatening semantics, such as saying the test has been "inconclusive" or "borderline." I took their advice.

I now put patients with similar problems in touch with one another. One of my patients had had open-heart surgery. Another was about to. Getting them together gave the second patient a larger dimension of understanding about the procedure, and he approached it with greater confidence.

Also as a result of a feedback discussion, I instituted a new telephone practice. When patients call in a non-critical situation—to find out results of some tests, for example—my staff will pull their charts and I'll call them back at the end of the day. This all but eliminates interruptions when I'm with patients in the office. And feedback inspired my procedure mentioned earlier of having patients phone ahead to see if I'm running late in my appointments and thereby save themselves needless waiting.

Such changes might be suggested by medical management experts. But when suggested by a patient, more than procedure is involved. A patient who feels that an office process has changed because of something he said at a feedback session knows he is being taken seriously. From that point on he'll be much more involved in his medical care.

I've increased my follow-up efforts whenever I send a patient to another physician—largely because of an episode at one of my feedback sessions. One of my patients reported she'd gone to the doctor, waited several hours, and then been poorly treated.

"Why didn't you tell me?" I asked.

"What good would it have done? I only went there once, I'd already come and gone."

"I'll tell you what good it would have done. Since I referred you to that doctor, I've referred several other patients to him. Had I known what happened to you, I would've spoken with him—and possibly sent my patients to another physician."

When patients have complained about a few specialists at feedback sessions, I've called those doctors, told them about my meetings, and indicated what patients had to say about them. They made concrete changes as a result: patients more warmly greeted; seen at the scheduled hour; been promptly told of their doctors' findings.

There comes a point in the feedback when I try to sum up what's happened and underscore what's relevant to my patients' health-maintenance.

"We constantly have to judge the physician," I usually begin. "You may make a good choice of physician in 1975, but things may happen to you or the physician that may make that choice not as good by 1979. You think of yourselves as powerless patients who can't know. You must never doubt your ability to know. It may be beyond your ability to know the best in competence, but it's not beyond your ability to know what's better. You don't need an expert to tell you what's a good bedside manner. *You know when you're being mistreated.* If it doesn't *seem* right, then it just may not *be* right.

"That night that the doctor doesn't call back, call again, and again. There will come a time when unless you've developed the habit of being reasonably assertive, you won't be able to function this way when you need to. If you're with a doctor who doesn't answer questions, no matter how competent he is, he's still a poor choice for a doctor. If you're afraid to call him, then no matter how competent he is, he's shut you off from his competence.

"If ever I or anyone else puts you into an unpleasant or alienating or dehumanizing situation, I want you to let me know. If you require warmth anc concern in your family doctor, there's no reason why you should tolerate anything less in specialists you're referred to. You shouldn't accept less because it's a one-shot deal. The specialist should ease your fears by explaining the procedure and setting aside misconceptions and half-truths. Just as I'm able to judge his competence, you're able to judge his warmth. We're all specialists in knowing how we react to someone—including a doctor.

"To the degree you don't judge, to the degree

you're not informed, to the degree I don't communicate well with you or you don't communicate well with me, to the degree you're upset with me and don't let me know, or vice versa, the quality of care we'd both like to see will not be possible. *It's a mutual responsibility. It's not all me. It's not my job, not your job. It's our job."*

Patient behavior doesn't automatically change in three hours. But the feedback session does alert patients to some of my expectations for them, and to the desirability of asserting themselves. They begin to know more about the mechanics of the office. They become aware of patients' rights. But the feedback won't automatically change the way they react to illness and its symptoms.

The feedback is a beginning. It informs. It sets a mood. It gives clues to what's possible. But nothing more will happen unless a patient encounters a consistent, pervading climate throughout the relationship that reemphasizes the values first limned in the feedback.

The feedback technique has a flexible format. It can vary with the practice or the physician or the group. It can vary in setting, time, place. The basic requirement is to meet in small groups, and to examine in an open, self-critical manner the doctor-patient relationship.

What's in it for physicians?

Feedback sessions increase patient cooperation

and satisfaction. They diminish patient turnover, a disheartening problem for doctors. They increase the familiarity of the patient with the problems of the doctor. And by increasing the time they spend with the patient in a feedback program they may very well save time in the end. Patients call the doctor because they're confused and worried. The feedback begins to answer some of their questions and offset some of their needless worries.

And for the patients? They can reveal their upset and continue the relationship without it having to fester and rupture. They will improve the quality of their care. They'll understand more and be able to cooperate more. And they'll not be as discouraged when change doesn't happen as quickly as they'd like.

One of the greatest rewards is that doctor and patient are open with one another. I didn't know the feelings of some of my patients until I started the feedback sessions. A patient would say to me, "You should have *known* I was angry with you." But it just isn't so easy to catch a hint or some nonverbal signal when you're focusing on a physical exam. The feedback gives the doctor a tool for discovering what his patients are like and what's on their minds. He probably can't ever fully know how a patient thinks. Even when he himself is a patient, he remains a doctor, viewing from the doctor's perception. Only through some kind of verbal interaction can he begin to comprehend what a pa-

tient thinks about specialists, hospitals, drugs—
and himself.

For the patient the change can be fundamental.
He can learn to see his doctor not as a god, but a
person.

9

Psychosocial Self-Help

AMERICA'S HEALTH profile speaks for itself. There are more than nine million alcoholics in the United States, and alcohol abuse is involved in more than half of the fifty thousand auto-pedestrian fatalities per year, according to the *Journal of the American Medical Association*. More than fifty million smokers consume $8 billion worth of tobacco yearly, according to the *New England Journal of Medicine*. Thirty percent of adults are markedly overweight; obesity is a major factor in one out of ten deaths, according to figures in the *Annals of Internal Medicine*. The correlation between exercise and health is incontestable, yet the overwhelming majority of Americans don't even own a pair of sneakers. As a nation, we are over-

eaters, underexercisers, worriers, and indulgers—
prime candidates for disease.

Despite the advances of science and medicine,
the life span has not been extended in the last
twenty to twenty-five years. Much work has been
done to improve one's chances of living to forty
or forty-five, but no progress has been made in
extending life beyond that time. That is, a forty-
five-year-old man in 1950 stood just as good a
chance of living to seventy as does a forty-five-year-
old man today. Cardiovascular diseases, heart attacks, cancer, strokes, and neurological diseases
have arrested longevity prospects.

To understand why this has happened, we must
look to the *psychosocial* causes of disease.

In spite of possible genetic tendencies, it is the
interplay with the environment that determines
the clinical, outward, harmful expression of disease.
Not everyone exposed to virus gets a disease. Resistance is the key. Even those exposed and infected
with what is called "subclinical" polio or hepatitis
do not show overt clinical manifestations if their
resistance is strong. Yet the disease has infected
them, as shown by evidence of antibodies in the
blood and tissue.

When immunity fails, *why* does it fail? At least
part of the failure is psychosocial.

The psychosocial theory of disease holds that it
is no longer sufficient to define a patient in terms

of his illness. He must be defined in terms of the environment that produced the illness: his job, his activity or lack of it, his eating habits, his indulgences, and the ecological setting in which he functions.

Personality factors act as aggravating tendencies in conditions of hypertension, ulcers, asthma, and coronary artery disease.

Almost any disease may be an expression of stress. There may be a disease behind the symptom, as well. But frequently, stress alone can account for the symptoms. Here are some of the more common ones:

> Diarrhea
> Constipation
> Frequent urination
> Burning sensation while urinating
> Chest pain
> Headache
> Dizzy spells
> Nausea
> Heartburn
> Pain in joints
> Skin problems
> Palpitations
> Cough
> Shortness of breath

Stress is an inevitable aspect of being alive, but how do we handle it? Do we overschedule? Do we allow ourselves to be pressured? Or do we attempt to conserve the natural resources of our body?

All organs need rest, all bodily systems relief. We function cyclically. When personality factors keep us at the highest level of function, without rest, it's contrary to nature.

Leisure time is often misused. Instead of exercising in a noncompetitive way, we become embroiled in matches of all kinds; instead of releasing tension, we actually increase tension.

Exercise is a way of relieving psychosocial stress. It keeps the body strong, prevents disease, and maintains health. Exercise is any increase in physical activity; it doesn't necessarily require independent time; it can be integrated into your day:

> Take stairs instead of the elevator.
> Walk a little farther.
> Walk a little faster.
> Stand often.
> Stretch and turn.
> Lift something heavy once a day.

Every time you move, you "spend" calories. Each day your weight is determined mostly by the amount of calories you consume. If you consume more than you spend, you accumulate weight. If you're overweight, you're putting a needless load on your heart. The smart patient spends calories to buy health.

EATING FOR HEALTH

Many diseases can be prevented by avoiding certain foods. A proper nutritional approach early in life cuts down the tendency to such diseases as diabetes and high blood pressure. Poor nutrition, conversely, or the habitual consumption of certain foods can be damaging.

We know that cancer of the stomach is common in Japan, due, possibly to the frequent use of smoked and raw fish. We know that cancer of the esophagus is much more prevalent in cultures that use hot liquids and spicy and smoked foods.

There's highly suggestive evidence that in underdeveloped countries where more grains, nuts, and seeds are consumed and processed foods are unheard of, there is less cancer of the colon, and less hiatus hernia, hemorrhoids, gallbladder disease, or hardening of the arteries. Stools pass through the colon much more quickly, and in greater bulk.

Salt can be deadly. We can medically survive on one to two grams of salt a day, but we eat more than ten to twelve grams a day. Excess salt intake is associated with hypertension and high blood pressure. As we age, our bodies' capacity to tolerate salt diminishes; we absorb and retain more salt, which promotes heart and kidney failure.

When we subject our bodies to such overloads, even early in life, we are laying the groundwork for trouble in later years.

Taste is learned. In Africa, tribes near salt licks are accustomed to having salty foods. Tribes away from salt licks can't tolerate salty foods.

But taste can be changed. Using spices and herbs in cooking can soon diminish our taste for salt to controllable and tolerable levels. We can reduce our consumption of salted packaged foods: pretzels, nuts, ham, bacon, frankfurters, delicatessen appetizers, herring, and pickles. By slowly reducing our salt intake, we have a greater likelihood of changing our tastes—particularly if the reduction is accompanied by an increase in the use of such appetite enhancers as onions, pepper, and herbs. If you feel your resolve is weakening, recall what the *Wall Street Journal* pointed out in a recent article —that we are so accustomed to processed chemicalized food we reject natural tastes. In other words, food processors have addicted us to their products. That should convince you to eat natural foods.

Sugar: We eat more refined sugar, measured by calories, than any other country—including the countries that grow sugar cane. Excess sugar contributes to diabetes, hardening of the arteries, stomach and intestinal disorders. There is plenty of sweetness in fresh fruits like melon and berries, and in dried fruits such as raisins, figs, and dates. Natural carbohydrates like potatoes, corn, peas, and rice are much better for you than prepared foods like puddings, pies, cakes, and cookies, all of which contain refined sugar.

There is evidence that increase in fat calories in the last fifty to sixty years is intimately related to arteriosclerosis, epidemic heart disease, cerebrovascular disease, and circulation problems. Studies of populations who emigrated to the United States from Scandinavia and the Orient demonstrate a changing pattern of disease after they adapt to diets in the United States that feature beef, pork, and dairy products. Studies of Seventh Day Adventists, who eat no red meats and emphasize roughage in their diet, show infrequent cases of hypertension, arterial disease, cancer of the colon, or digestive disturbances.

Those cultural groups who live the longest share certain nutritional habits:

> They eat no foods with chemicals, additives and preservatives.
> They eat no processed foods.
> They use little salt, preferring more natural herbs and spices.
> They use little or no refined sugars.
> They use little or no fats in their diets— particularly saturated fats.
> They use very little red meat or shellfish, emphasizing, instead, fresh fish, chicken, turkey and veal.

Are you interested in extending your life? There's your menu.

Foods that are preserved, salted, and highly chemicalized are prepared in this fashion for convenience, not for health. Convenience-packaged food and fast-food restaurants embody all the worst elements of nutrition.

A little extra shopping time is extra life time. You can always have fresh fruits, salads, and vegetables ready at hand. You can pass up the packaged, canned and bottled foods if, as is likely, they contain preservatives. Just take the time to look at the labels.

You cannot expect your doctor to be interested in you as a whole person unless you yourself are interested. It's up to you to approach the physician with a new strategy for health. Rather than coming in to talk only about a specific symptom, you should also bring information and thoughts about your day: how you slept, whether you felt pressured, what you've been eating, whether you're drinking coffee, what your job is like, who you're upset with, whether you feel frightened or anxious, or whether you feel driven to smoke.

If we accept that disease is related to psychosocial causes then we must acknowledge that it is we ourselves who have the opportunity to extend and safeguard our lives.

10

Open Medicine

HOW YOU receive and pay for medical care, as well as the nature of the care you receive, may change profoundly within the next decade.

You may become part of a health-maintenance organization—HMO—in which your needs are met by a number of doctors functioning as a group. Your own doctor may join such a group himself. Whether he does or not, it is increasingly likely that he will soon be asked to prove his proficiency to his peers every several years; such a requirement already exists for family practitioners. The health-consumer movement has taken hold across the country in recent years, and as it continues to expand, you will have an increasing opportunity to involve yourself in questions of public policy, standards, and the availability of care. Finally, in all likelihood, the cost of your medical care will soon be financed by a program of national health insurance. Your payments will be indirect, through taxes.

Between ten and twelve percent of the U.S. gross national product is now allocated for health care. Inevitably, as costs rise, as specialization increases, as the delivery of health care becomes more and more complex, and as the revolution of rising expectations increases demands for care, we have to achieve the economies that permit the scope of care to broaden. New means of delivery may raise the level of competence throughout the country, as well as distribute care more evenly through the various economic sectors. Great Britain has demonstrated that when cost ceases to be a factor in determining who shall have and not have treatment, the volume of people who seek care rises significantly. So we can look toward broader coverage. But what kind of care will it be?

Many people believe that as soon as the distribution of medical care is improved, its quality will automatically improve. I don't believe that is assured. As medical care comes to be dominated by third parties and federal bureaucracies, and as doctors and patients organize into groups, the question of whether care itself will improve will depend on the humanity in these new forms. If they become depersonalized, then however widespread the care, its quality will inevitably diminish.

As I've said, I can't solve economic problems, I can't affect technology. Where I can focus my concern is on the compassion that has to accompany care. Most everyone in this country gives a great deal of attention to the cost of medical care and its technology. But few authorities concern themselves with the ways in which we can safeguard and enhance medicine's human components. If we're not careful, humanity will be lost.

Whatever the potential problems, change is inevitable. An almost unending debate about our health delivery system has been under way for the last dozen years. The rise of health consumerism underscores public concern; the incredible increase in malpractice suits adds a note of urgency for all.

During the 1960s, malpractice suits numbered some six thousand a year. In 1973, the figure had more than doubled. One aspect underlying such suits is a conviction on the part of patients that they weren't fully informed about drugs or surgery or the consequences of treatment.

The malpractice suit arises from an emotional as well as physical hurt. It is a tragic commentary on a relationship between doctor and patient that has been characterized by abdication to the expert. When the patient is not informed, his expectations can be unrealistic. He can't give his informed consent because he hasn't the information on which to base it. The doctor, for his part, has demonstrated a lack of trust in the patient; if the doctor knew and cared for his patient, he would entrust him with knowledge. Studies have shown that where there's a warm, compassionate relationship characterized by respect and good communication, the rate of malpractice suits diminishes compared to those circumstances where physicians are abrupt and uncommunicative with patients.

Even where malpractice is not involved, we have seen how ignorance—whether caused by alienation, awe, fright, or any other aspect of the medical mystique—leads inevitably to poor quality care. As we face the increasing likelihood of assembly-line mass-produced health service, the vigilant, questioning, assertive patient becomes even more critically important to his own well-being.

Consider the nature of care under the health-maintenance organizations. They came into being because many physicians felt that by banding together they could reduce the soaring cost of medical care as well as raise its quality in many parts of the country. HMO type organizations have existed for some time. One of them, the Kaiser-Permanente Medical Care Program, has 2.3 million members in California and another 500,000 in Ohio, Colorado, Oregon, and Hawaii. Kaiser-Permanente has existed since 1942. The Health Insurance Plan of Greater New York (HIP) is more than thirty years old. Members of these organizations pay fees each month, but nothing out of pocket when there is medical need.

There are obvious advantages to groups: generally lower cost; more peer review; doctors in closer proximity, able to consult with one another at will; convenient consultations with specialists. And yet such programs may work adversely. Doctors may band together to protect one another. Salaries may diminish motivation; the doctor will be paid the same, however hard he works. Patients may find the group setup more intimidating; relationships may not be as intimate; assertiveness may become more difficult. Finally, the bigger the system, the more bureaucracy and the more barriers to direct communication with the doctor.

The vigilance of patients is more than ever necessary for another significant reason—as a social counterbalance to the increasing power of medicine in society. Doctors have powerful roles in defining what's right or wrong for people. As mentioned, they regulate the dispensing of drugs, certain forms of contraception, and abortion. They label certain forms of behavior "diseased." They determine who gets a kidney or a heart and who doesn't.

Doctors in hospitals throughout the United States are making decisions involving extension of life. Life can be prolonged with antibiotics, intravenous fluids, and breathing machines. Imagine a man who has lived a long and full and vigorous life but who is now totally helpless—paralyzed, unable to speak or see, alive only because of medicine and machines. The law says that his life must go on, and yet when he is asked, this man may say that he would prefer to die. I have heard this same circumstance described by doctors. What should the doctor do? My answer is that he should do nothing by himself. Do doctors have some special status that permits them to make those kinds of judgments? I recall the story of one doctor who solved the problem by summoning the patient's family and his minister. They concurred that the patient, whom they knew intimately and loved deeply, would not wish to continue life in this state. They put the question to him. He understood and confirmed their judgment. Only then did the doctor carry out his wish. To have a doctor make such a decision alone in the patient's behalf is to let the doctor play God.

New techniques are being developed to help persons with behavior problems caused by chemical or structural changes in their brains. But behavior is an inherent part of self, and certain forms of behavior modification and psychosurgery may be potential violations of the individual's identity. Shall the doctor, any more than any other authority, determine what treatment is appropriate?

Transplant surgeons have developed an extraordinary skill. They offer life to persons who would die without their help. But is it for them to determine when a donor is dead, or which recipient should receive an organ?

This is not to say that, up to this point, doctors' decisions have not been good ones, or that medicine has used its powers injudiciously. But such influence solely in the hands of doctors makes the public increasingly uncomfortable. The corrective is social pressure. But will it be forthcoming? The public has been so indoctrinated with the notion that doctors are people set apart that it is, in effect, in a cultural constraint.

So that there can be no misunderstanding of the specific dimension of my concern, I repeat: Most of the physicians I know are caring and competent craftsmen. Nonetheless, even among this group —and I include myself among them—there are times when the medical mystique inevitably enters into the relationship with patients. To the degree that it does we are behaving in a way that impairs our intentions to deliver the best possible care.

And in the larger social context, we are subtly but surely reinforcing the role of medicine as a social controller. As long as individual patients do not achieve an adult, assertive relationship with their doctors, they will never challenge medicine's social functions. Until that challenge is vigorously made, society will remain in the thrall of the medical mystique.

Obviously the place to start is with the individual patient, building his confidence to function within the arena of medicine.

That is really what my feedback sessions are about: to make patients comfortable with our relationship, to move them away from blind reliance on someone else's judgment.

I try to provide my patients an opportunity and setting in which they can judge me. Sometimes they judge me harshly. Sometimes, I feel, they misjudge me. But whether they criticize me or praise me, they come to understand that they have a capacity to judge—and that I am not a god to worship.

For my part, I have trust and confidence in their intelligence, their humanity, and their ability to participate. The objective of a feedback session, as I've said, is not to be a gripe session with the doctor but to give patients the familiarity and confidence to work with me toward their own better health.

To achieve that fully, we have to move beyond the feedback into a setting that is an unfamiliar one to our time but a familiar one to history; to the doctor as educator, the patient as student, and the medical work setting as an arena for learning.

The Scientists' Institute for Public Information has declared, "The promise of modern technology for mankind is matched by its threat. Unheeding use of the enormous powers science has given us is already seriously stressing both the social fabric and the ecological system in which we live. We cannot declare a moratorium on the progress of science. The real question is: Can our society learn responsible use of the knowledge and powers that science provides? The answer can be yes, but only in a world where both statesmen and voters understand the implications of science for their own lives and communities. Only a public that knows both the benefits and risks of present and proposed technologies can weigh these benefits and risks and make responsible choices about how science will be applied to their lives."

To effect such change, the Institute has set itself up as a clearinghouse for science information and a coordinating body for affiliated local science information committees.

What's the prospect for medicine informing the public in similar fashion?

Medical schools could make a significant contribution by sensitizing young doctors to the need to communicate with and educate patients. Medical societies and specialty groups could do much the same with their members, using seminars and conventions for courses in how to communicate with patients. But while both efforts would be enormously helpful, neither one attacks the problem at its root. The problem begins in the doctor-patient relationship. It's in the solving of this problem that medicine has its greatest opportunity: to move the doctor-patient relationship from a disease base to a health base.

Health education is a disaster in America.

Ninety-four cents of the national health dollar is spent on treatment of disease; four cents is spent on research; two cents is spent on preventive medicine, of which four-tenths of a cent is for health education. Most Americans get their disease-prevention information in a casual way: their knowledge about cholesterol, as one example, depends about totally on whether they happened to see an article about it in a newspaper or magazine. And yet they may be shortening their lives by eating cholesterol-producing food.

Formal health education, such as it is, is delivered as part of hygiene or physical education classes in high school, and then promptly forgotten. Histories of health education make no mention of what is potentially its most significant and natural arena—the patient-physician encounter in the normal medical work setting—the doctor's office.

Patients are taught to think of doctors almost exclusively in terms of disease and sickness. Health goes far beyond disease. It concerns itself with positive life styles that build barriers against disease. What is there in a patient's life that may make him ill *in the future?*

Many, I suspect, tend to perceive the medical profession in the abstract as composed of individuals primarily motivated by a desire to earn money, and who basically give indifferent care to patients and rush them through with little attention to their feelings. As patients, though, we have a much different feeling about our personal physician. I believe the explanation for this discrepancy is found, once again, in the mystique. Doctors in the abstract personify the negative mystique. Doctors in the specific often do utilize the healing charisma of the mystique: its leadership and teaching aspects. To the degree that the positive aspect of the mystique is in play, patient cynicism tends to diminish.

Many doctors complain that it's difficult to motivate patients to adopt good health habits. But if such doctors asked for change from their patients in the context of their own efforts to change, the results might be quite different. Some doctors' protests notwithstanding, the research strongly suggests that where a doctor makes a determined effort in behalf of good health habits, he does have a significant impact. *The American Journal of Public Health* carried a comparison several years ago of two groups—one that had and one that hadn't been involved in discussions with their doctors about how to reduce smoking. Only nine percent of the second group reduced its smoking, whereas thirty-three percent of those who had the benefit of information and guidance from their doctors was able to cut down.

As a rule you probably react to what happens rather than to what *might* happen. When you smoke and nothing happens, you tend not to be concerned about the cancer you're risking. Not surprisingly, you tend not to take into account the time required before the onset of pain. It's been suggested that if drinkers would get a hangover after the first drink instead of the next morning, the problem of alcoholism would be solved. Still, if you're thoroughly informed of the consequences of helpful versus harmful health behavior, I believe you can and will respond in your own self-interest.

The time you spend waiting in a doctor's office is a "teachable moment." You're primed to consider your well-being. Some argue that a patient who isn't feeling well is in no mood to be taught. But often you aren't feeling poorly when you come to see your doctor. And rarely do you feel so badly you're unable to talk or ask questions. To the contrary, because you feel you're with someone with special knowledge who can help you, your receptivity is probably heightened.

Some doctors have made a practice of giving patients literature to read at home. An excellent practice. But why stop there? Why not use the doctor's office as an educational room? Why not fill it with teaching aids—and have a qualified person on hand to supervise and coordinate the education?

Health education requires the full utilization of

the techniques and skills of the communicating arts, including not only pamphlets, films, graphics, slides, but audiovisual aids, video cassettes and disks, closed-circuit TV, and audio cassette recordings. Such technology has been used widely to sell the commodities of industry; the time has long passed when a prime human commodity—health —should have been wedded to these most modern communication techniques.

But merely putting somebody in front of electronic devices is not enough. Most of us need a human presence to guide and motivate us. Often that person can't be the doctor. It has to be the health educator, a trained member of the medical team.

"Health educators" are among the newest of specialists in the world of medicine. Many are PhDs employed mostly in larger groups, such as HMOs or health agencies. They are to medicine today what the physiotherapist was to the medical profession only a few years ago. Then, physical therapists had limited acceptance. Doctors and patients alike were dubious about the therapeutic effects of their baths, massages, diathermy, and ultrasonic treatments. Today, there are few orthopedists who don't have physical therapists working with them.

The physician remains the focal point of medical care. It's in his office where health educators belong.

Skilled educational therapists could be easily recruited from the large number of allied health professionals who, with training, could function in a teaching capacity.

These "information therapists" would be knowledgeable in health education and behavioral science, medicine and nutrition. They could lecture on sex, sleep, diet, obesity, coffee drinking, alcohol, smoking, and exercise. They could offer a positive program for health. They could take up many of the subjects that are first ventilated in feedback sessions, and develop them more fully: patient behavior and what influences it, how to recognize the symptoms, how to examine doctors, how to talk to them, how to function in hospitals.

There's so much you could learn from such professionals to improve life. Just one example: Suppose you have a persistent headache. Sleep won't help. Aspirin does nothing. The headache lasts for weeks. Obviously, you must be examined. You may even need to see a neurologist. Your emotional stresses must be looked into. The possibility of a brain tumor must be considered. But what may finally be discovered is that nothing is medically wrong—except that you don't know how to control the humidification in your room. A room that's too dry will give you a headache. You'd have been spared enormous pain and expense and time if you'd learned this from an available health educator.

Today the health educators are trying to get their services paid for by insurance carriers in the same way these carriers now pay for physiotherapy. In the long run, everyone would save money.

A few billion dollars spent to teach you and other Americans to develop a life style conducive to good health—and when ill or disabled, to understand and cope more effectively with your own health problems—could turn out to be far more cost effective than billions spent on the development of exotic new medical technology and expensive in-patient programs.

You can make choices. You should be presented with options. I'm not asking you to become a surgeon or cardiologist, but rather an expert in knowing how to ask questions about what's being done to you. You can't possibly begin to get rid of the medical mystique until you acquire the knowledge and competence to be able to evaluate your physician. That is the prerequisite to open medicine.

What I'm asking for is something in concert with the best of American values, the promotion of self-reliance and self-discovery, and an emphasis on learning. We Americans are innovative and action-oriented. These attributes are part of our natural resources. We need to use them to solve the social consequences of the medical mystique.

You have rights as a patient. Rights and responsibilities go together. You have the responsibility to exercise your rights. Once you do, in a spirit of openness, you will have achieved a vital partnership in your own health enterprise.